Praise for *Soul Recovery*

"Rather than a book based on echoes of inspirational ideas, Ester Nicholson's extraordinary work is a sharing of personal experience as she moves from the darkness of futility to a rebirth of new life. This adventure of *Soul Recovery* follows a pathway of healing light with twelve keys as spiritual stepping-stones. It's a glorious journey in reshaping the mind for greater oneness with the Holiness within—and as that happens, miracles follow. Highly recommended."

—John Randolph Price, Bestselling author and
Chairman of the Quartus Foundation

"In this book, Ester Nicholson captures the power and promise of forgiveness for a community that desperately needs it. She shows how to expand the 12-Step process into a comprehensive spiritual teaching. I strongly recommend this book for anyone seeking their own Soul Recovery."

—Colin Tipping, Award-winning author of *Radical Forgiveness*

"*Soul Recovery* is a Godsend of compassionate understanding, grit and grace known by one who has victoriously walked the path."

—Michael Bernard Beckwith, Founder of Agape International
Spiritual Center and author of *Life Visioning*

"Ester Nicholson has all the essential qualities of greatness— a unique tone, wonderful phrasing, emotional flexibility and passion. In a nutshell the girl's got soul!"

—Rod Stewart, Grammy Award-winning singer-songwriter and
member of Rock and Roll Hall of Fame

"If you are searching for how to renew your mind and engage your spirit to move beyond white-knuckling being clean and sober, open this book and let it take you down a path to power, wholeness, and rich sustaining life."

—Stan Stokes MS, LPC, CAC, Founder & President of Bridging the Gaps, an Integrative Addictions Treatment Center

"Ester's life is one of transformation and redemption. In her hauntingly honest narrative about a life transformed and heartbreak transcended, she gives readers the 12 Keys to do this in their own lives."

—Julie Silver, MD, Assistant Professor, Harvard Medical School and author of *You Can Heal Yourself*

"*Soul Recovery* shows that true and lasting happiness comes from a deeper understanding of one's Self and a deeper well-spring of being."

—Velvet Mangan, CEO of Safe Harbor Treatment Centers for Women

SOUL
RECOVERY

12 Keys to Healing Addiction

. . . And Twelve Steps for the Rest of Us—
a Path to Wholeness, Serenity and Success

ESTER NICHOLSON

Foreword by Michael Bernard Beckwith

Agape Media International

Agape Media International

Published by
Agape Media International, LLC
5700 Buckingham Parkway
Culver City, California 90230
310.258.4401
www.agapeme.com

HAY HOUSE

Distributed by
Hay House, Inc.
P.O. Box 5100, Carlsbad, CA 92018-5100
(760)-431-7695 or (800)-654-5126

Hay House USA: *www.hayhouse.com*
Hay House UK: *www.hayhouse.co.uk*
Hay House Australia: *www.hayhouse.com.au*
Hay House South Africa: *www.hayhouse.co.za*
Hay House India: *www.hayhouse.co.in*

Soul Recovery — 12 Keys to Healing Addiction
Ester Nicholson
www.soulrecovery.org

Book Credits
Executive In Charge Of Publication: Stephen Powers
Co-author: Ben Dowling
Editor: Rebecca Heyman
Design: Frame25 Productions
Photography: Maria Rangel
Back Cover Photograph: Maria Rangel
Interior Photograph, page 163: Penny Lancaster-Stewart

Printed in USA on recycled paper.
ISBN: 978-1401943110

For those standing on the edge of their breakthrough, ready to leap into the knowledge, understanding and embodiment of their true nature that has always been wholeness.

TABLE OF CONTENTS

PREFACE

"I've done it again."

I'd been getting high for most of the afternoon, and had told my daughter to stay in her room and watch television. She came out of the room several times, wanting my attention and her dinner. I gave her some crackers and cookies instead. This was not the first time.

She gave up trying to get my attention or her dinner and finally fell asleep. At about three in the morning, when all the drugs were gone and I was totally sprung, I took my last twenty dollars and woke her up to walk with me around the corner to the drug dealer's house. I just needed one more hit, then I'd be done. She was sleepy and whining. My heart said, "Don't do this. This is screwed up. You're such a mess. What kind of mother are you?" But I was not in control; the insatiable hunger and cravings for more were my master, and I had to obey. So we walked out into the dark, chilly pre-dawn hours. The streets were deathly quiet. It felt like all the people in the world were snuggled cozily in their beds, while I was out walking the streets with my seven-year-old daughter to score more drugs.

We arrived at the drug dealer's house. The scent of the place assaulted me as soon as he opened the door. There was a broken-down couch in the living room. I think the color used to be gold, but it was so filthy I couldn't tell. Scattered around the room were two or three wooden chairs with the stuffing pulled out of the seat cushions, and God knows what kind of stains on the carpet. The house smelled like cigarettes, free-base, rum, sex and filth. Of course, that didn't mean anything to me then. I just needed one more hit.

I gave the drug dealer my last twenty and he gave me the drugs. I sat there and smoked away my daughter's food money for the next day. When I was through and the drugs were gone, the realization of having spent my very last dime dawned on me. I was panicked, frustrated and full of remorse, and the overwhelming feeling of "Oh, God...I've done it again."

My frightened little daughter and I eventually left, walking down the street at 4 AM. The shame came pouring out of me, and I cried hysterically over and over again, "Mommy will never do it again, baby. I'm so sorry." She looked at me with hope and disbelief all at once, even at her young age. She'd heard this promise before. She already knew we'd come this way again.

And we did.

FOREWORD

When we think of addiction—whether it involves drugs, alcohol, sex, shopping, social media, food, work, exercise, ideologies—we are most frequently referring to that which has become an obsession for filling the empty spaces within our lives, within our hearts, that which appears to alleviate stress, to anesthetize the pain of anxiety, loss, fear, a sense of not-enoughness. Certainly that was once true in Ester Nicholson's life. For years I witnessed her journey from releasing life-constricting habits to embodying the life-transforming practices she vulnerably and generously shares in this book.

Within the mind are the seeds of personal self-destruction as well as self-transformation. The day-to-day, moment-by-moment choices we make determine which seed will bloom. There is an old Cherokee legend that aptly illustrates this point. It's said that a grandfather sat with his grandson teaching him skillful means for navigating life. "A fight is going on inside me," he shared with the boy. "It is a terrible fight between two wolves. One is evil—he is anger, envy, sorrow, regret, greed, arrogance, self-pity, guilt, resentment, inferiority, lies, false pride, superiority, and ego." He went on, "The other is good—he is joy, peace, love, hope, serenity, humility, kindness, benevolence, empathy, generosity, truth, compassion and faith." The grandson was pensive for a moment and then asked his grandfather, "Which wolf will win?" The grandfather wisely replied, "The one you feed."

When we don't know how to create change from within, we reach outside of ourselves and become attached to that which appears to provide instant relief. The word "attachment" comes from the French "attaché," meaning "nailed to," and is used in Eastern spiritual traditions to describe how we obsessively bite the hook of attachment, be it a substance or habitual action, even to religion or "do-gooding." By practicing the principles described in this book, you will reclaim your innate empowerment and capacity to feed the life-affirming Self within you. Expanding into this sense of Self is a core human impulse that enables you to handle life's challenges from an expansive perspective.

Ester's inspired 12-Key Path is the result of her inner work in consciousness. As you accompany her in the chapters that follow, you will soon realize that what she offers is not mere theory but rather a result of her direct experience of self-transformation, of choosing to feed the "good wolf" within. *Soul Recovery* is a Godsend of compassionate understanding, grit and grace known by one who has victoriously walked the path. The fact that you have picked up this book implies that at some level of your being you are already setting your intention for the changes you envision. Know for certain that absolutely nothing stands in your way of taking action on that intention.

Michael Bernard Beckwith
Founder, Agape International Spiritual Center
and author of *Life Visioning*

INTRODUCTION

I have written this book in order to take you from powerlessness to a place of shining in your full power.

That may seem impossible to you right now or, at best, a hopeful dream of a future you would like to have. If you are struggling with addiction, feeling peaceful and powerful in a real way that is connected to Source, to God, and to the depths of your own being can feel farther away than you are even capable of imagining.

But I am here to show you—with my story and my recovery—that finding your power again is possible. It will depend on your own ability to be humble in the face of the demons you are fighting right now. But because you had the humility to pick up this book, I know you are ready to reclaim that power—even if you are in the darkest place of your life.

I wrote this book because I believe in you. I believe you can escape the chains of addiction. In fact, I know you can. I am your ally, standing beside you, shining a light on the path that leads out of the nightmare of addiction. When you read the stories set out in this book, you will read about events that might sound like they could have come from your own life. That is why I want you to pay attention to what happens next, because I had a complete healing from my addiction and I am here to guide you to yours.

It is possible. Keep reading.

This is a book about recovery—my recovery—from addiction to drugs, specifically cocaine. But, as anyone with the mind of an addict knows, my addictions didn't stop there. I was addicted to filling the bottomless pit of my broken heart and hungry soul with anything and everything external to myself—drugs, love, men, food, you name it—if it gave me the temporary illusion of feeling whole and complete, even if only for an instant. My wants knew no end. Those wants nearly destroyed me and my child many, many times over.

But I rose like a phoenix from those ashes. I rose to claim my true power. And God responded. Call it the Universe, call it Spirit, call it whatever—I am referring to that great and all-knowing power that has created us all.

My name is Ester, and I am a powerful, magnificent, whole, perfect and complete expression of Spirit. That has always been my true identity. And it is also yours.

But I forgot. It's easy to forget.

My early upbringing taught me that I was powerless, unworthy, not enough—and I bought it.

The fear, unworthiness and shame I felt were so much a part of my identity that it was as if they were in my very bone marrow. I couldn't tell where these feelings left off and I began. I couldn't separate myself from the fiction I had identified with for so long. That story had been repeated over and over until it seemed like it was true. But it wasn't true. It never was.

Just getting off the drugs didn't stop the patterns that were distorting my vision. Getting clean didn't heal my crazy, obsessive thinking. The issues that had led me to the drugs in the first place were still running my life, even after I got sober.

So what was missing?

As much as I had recovered, I was still the walking wounded, bleeding from the inside out—as if slashed to ribbons by the fearful thought patterns and beliefs I had taken on as my reality.

I want you to get this, because this is at the heart of your healing, too. The keys to your Soul's recovery go deeper than just getting clean and sober.

Even after over a decade of sobriety and working the 12 Steps with the desperation of a dying woman, I still had trouble accepting that I was worthy of good, even when amazing opportunities like appearing on *The Oprah Show*, *The Ellen Degeneres Show* and *The View* were happening in my life. Why was I still broke when I was earning more money than I had ever imagined? Why was I still looking—no, begging—for love in all the wrong places? Why was I still filled with fear about everything?

The answer was that I hadn't healed my self-worth.

The 12 Steps got me as far as they could take me. They got me to sobriety and for that I will be eternally grateful. But I wrote this book because I believe there are layers of our wounded thought patterns and beliefs that the 12 Steps are simply not designed to heal.

In the beginning of the recovery process, we are all like infants—learning to roll over, stand up and walk. The purpose of the 12 Steps is to stand us up and prepare us to meet our true selves as expressions of God.

I am a living testament that the 12 Steps of Alcoholics Anonymous are extremely powerful. They were the steps I required in the immediate crisis of drug/alcohol and food addiction. But there came a time in my healing when the Steps were no longer enough for me. I needed to take the power greater than myself out of the sky, the churches and AA meetings, and connect it to myself in a more tangible way.

The 12 Steps brought me to the realization that I was powerless and that my life was unmanageable, in order that I could be humble enough to truly listen, grow and find a new direction.

After years of practicing the principles I learned in the 12 Steps—turning my life over to God and experiencing a direct connection to that power—the strangest thing happened: I realized that the power of God was not greater than me.

I realized that it *was* me.

Oh, what a revelation; what a breakthrough! I couldn't continue to affirm my powerlessness according to the 12 Steps because I no longer believed I was separate and apart from the source of Life itself. This changed everything. Many recovering addicts make all the right motions—attend meetings, memorize the readings, talk to their sponsors—yet never actually reach their full recovery. I call this "healing from the outside in," because it works on the surface of the problem without achieving any permanent change. But by identifying my own life as an aspect of God's, I could heal "from the inside out"—which didn't just support my recovery from drugs, it recovered my wholeness as an expression of God Itself.

The ideas and the practices I developed from that point on are what inspired and birthed what I now call *Soul Recovery: 12 Keys to Healing Addiction*. It is a process designed to access the incredible inner power that resides in all of us.

When you are consciously connected to your inherent power, you are restored to balance, harmony and order. Cravings and out-of-balance behaviors simply dissolve in the face of it, because you are no longer operating at the "vibrational frequency" of powerlessness. You are operating in concert with the highest vibration that there is.

Now, I understand and recognize that clinical and psychiatric approaches to addiction can be very useful. I know people whose lives have been changed—and saved—because of therapy. But for someone like me, who came into this world already haunted by a thousand forms of fear, whose illusions of separation from her inner Spirit were so profound and whose experience was beset by violence, pain, addiction and one crisis after another—therapy is simply not enough. Church is not enough. Nor is the simple recitation of "think positive" affirmations enough.

This book tells my story: a story of a broken, wounded and seemingly powerless girl and how she was restored. It is a story about how to use the 12 Keys to heal. It is a book about transcending the "story" of being a victim in order to create a new life of balance, order and harmony, even in the midst of difficulty and challenge.

Because if I can, you can.

As you read, understand that Soul Recovery isn't about attaining perfection, but is about reclaiming your inherent wholeness. I will present to you a process that connects you to the power within—a power that is already perfect. It is through the realization of that inherent order and perfection that you will be able to meet challenges with a sense of freedom, peace and worthiness. It is a process that uncovers the magnificence that you already are, and prepares you for the amazing life you deserve.

While the 12 Keys can be utilized by anyone on the journey of recovering their wholeness, I wrote this book particularly for those still in the throes of a torn and injured existence of addictive behavior—drug addiction, love addiction, food addiction, domestic violence, child abuse and worse. Even if you're not sure, I know that at your core, you are whole. And I am convinced that my story and the processes I've developed can help you to realize this inherent wholeness.

Soul Recovery and the 12 Keys gave me back my life by providing a mountain-top view of reality beyond anything I had experienced before. The 12 Keys expanded my awareness beyond being free from addiction, to living in a state of mental freedom I never knew was possible. The teaching uncovered in me the hidden splendor of self-esteem, empowerment and self-love in a way that I thought was for other people, but not for me. This is how I know it is possible for you.

Working with and embodying the 12 Keys continues to support me in staying awake to that all-pervading truth.

And it can do the same for you.

I love you,
Ester Nicholson

SOUL RECOVERY
THROUGH METAPHYSICS

This book uses concepts that are straight out of metaphysics.

The way I use the term "metaphysics" relates to the philosophical study of the nature of being—how our thoughts interact with the experiences we have in life. It deals with the realm of the invisible reality outside the confines and limitations of our five senses. It is also the study of "cause and effect," and how that mechanism works in our lives.

I've found that metaphysical teachings are empowering because they are based on the idea that you are the driver of your experience—that the power to change resides within you, not from somewhere outside of you.

Recognizing that you have the power to define and determine your experience is essential to affecting the conditions of your life, because otherwise you are at the mercy of your addictions, your problems, your human frailties and the world around you.

Metaphysics teaches that the quality of your life and the experiences you have are a direct result of your beliefs about life and your relationship with yourself. So, in a practical sense, the external conditions of your life hold up a mirror so you can see the dominant thoughts and beliefs that you hold in your awareness.

Beliefs are powerful. In fact, they are the creative foundation of your experience in life.

Most people don't know that. To be perfectly honest, I spent most of my life not knowing that. I thought that life was happening to me, rather than happening through me according to my thoughts and beliefs.

Soul Recovery is based on the idea that the "power greater than ourselves" is actually our true self. You are one with it— and it is through that realization that you can shift or heal your thinking, which in turn changes your experience of life. My life has certainly demonstrated that, and I want to share with you the specific tools that made healing possible for me and have the potential to do the same for you.

In Soul Recovery, a way of life becomes available to you that is radically different from the way you've been taught and the way that you've lived in the past. This model of recovery will provide the path to your healing. The way it expresses through you will be unique, because you are unique.

Just so you know ahead of time, I will use the term "God" a lot. But I want you to associate that word with an infinite source of energy and good, not a man in the sky. You can think of God as the power that holds matter and energy in a physical system, or as an infinite love that pervades all things.

I don't think God would have a problem with any of those.

HOW THIS BOOK WORKS

Of course, you've heard of the 12 Step Programs of Alcoholics Anonymous and other recovery programs. This book builds upon those initial tools by adding a Key that corresponds to each of the 12 Steps—hence, 12 Keys.

These 12 Keys draw on spiritual principles that are designed to heal your mind and your life.

I personally found it necessary to build on the 12 Keys for my own spiritual growth. This is what healed me, not just of addiction, but of the latent addictive tendencies I struggled to control, even in sobriety.

The Soul Recovery process is presented here as a 12-week course of study and practice. Each Key progresses from a basic teaching into the practices and actions that prepare you for the next Key. Of course, you don't have to compress your process into 12 weeks if that doesn't serve you. Some Keys require deeper work before moving on. I suggest you use your intuition to lead you here. You will know when you are ready to embrace the next Key.

Although each Key can be practiced outside of any particular order, I have found that taking each Key in turn provides the greatest benefit—particularly if this is the first time you are engaging in the Soul Recovery process.

During these 12 weeks, use the Keys every day. If you are in a 12 Step Program, the Keys are a perfect counterpoint to the vital lessons contained in the Steps. You will find as you delve more deeply into your spirituality and your connection to God that the Keys apply to a broad spectrum of human experience, providing a sense of freedom and empowerment.

Setting Intention

Each Key's work will start with setting an intention. An intention is "something that somebody plans to do or achieve" or "the state of having a purpose in mind."

The use of intention in our work serves two main purposes: firstly, it focuses our attention by identifying a clear context for each Key; and secondly, it helps us be aware of when our beliefs may be standing in the way of that context.

For example, your intention in the first of the 12 Keys is to realize a Universal Presence that is everywhere, and that you are one with it.

Might as well start big, right?

By establishing this clear intention, we are providing a context for our work within that Key: a divinely inspired context of freedom, balance, harmony, peace, love, abundance, joy, health and wholeness that is present in all things—including you. This intention also has the potential to rub up against some of our beliefs about God and about life—pointing out where we have work to do.

Contemplation

In each Key, you will focus on several "contemplations" that point your mind in a new direction.

The purpose of each contemplation is to take you into a deeper realization of your wholeness—no matter the conditions and history of your life.

Sometimes contemplations will get a little uncomfortable. You may be challenging long-held beliefs, including beliefs about who you are and how you came to be that way. When you embark on a deep spiritual journey, old ideas must die in order for new ones to arise. This cycle of death and rebirth can be very challenging.

Journaling

As you work with the 12 Keys, it's important to journal the feelings and questions you have throughout the process. Your feelings and questions will undergo change as you progress through the exercises in this book. This is perfectly normal.

I've discovered that there's something very cathartic about writing my feelings down on paper. I've found that when I'm contemplating a new idea and I write down my thoughts and questions with an open mind, I make myself available to receive insights I never knew were possible.

In addition, as new insights reveal themselves, writing them down supports the embodiment of these ideas in a deeper way. This often gives a tangible and visible form to something that may have started off as an abstract idea.

Therefore, you will need a notebook to use for your work.

Affirmations

Each of the 12 Keys could be called an "affirmation" or "affirmative statement," which will be the focus of your study and practice.

An affirmation is a positive declaration designed to transform your thinking. Affirmations are stated in "present time"—as though the goal desired has already been achieved. This is because Life, God or Spirit is happening now—not in the future. As you affirm that the good desired is present now, you make yourself available for the immediate manifestation of that affirmative statement in your life.

Affirmations, whether positively or negatively stated, have the power to create our experience. Actually, anything that you state with conviction is a form of an affirmation because these thoughts—spoken with commitment and energy—actively structure your thinking.

The 12 Keys are positive, life-changing affirmations.

Action Steps

"Faith without works is dead."
—James 2:14-26

You can gain incredible insights and changes by contemplation and journaling, but what really allows for deep transformation are action steps that are in alignment with the principles you've contemplated and journaled about.

At the end of each segment, you will be given action steps to support your process.

Closing Thoughts

Closing Thoughts are my personal summary of the process you've just engaged in, plus some additional color and detail that describe how the teaching assists you to realize wholeness in your life.

Meditative Quotes

These quotes have provided me with insights during my own work. They are from people who have a profound commitment to spiritual practice—and are useful as reflections and meditations throughout your week.

HOW I SUGGEST YOU USE
THIS BOOK

- Read each chapter all the way through before participating in any exercises.

- Write some initial thoughts in your notebook.

- Read each chapter's "Key" several times.

- Make time for your Contemplation & Journaling.

- Speak your Affirmations several times while reading.

- Schedule time for the appropriate Action Steps.

- Use the Keys and Meditative Quotes throughout your week.

I thank you for your willingness to join me on this extraordinary path to self-realization. This work will heal you at a profound level, freeing you to live again and realize the greatness and power that you are.

Your commitment to practicing these principles makes an emphatic statement to the Universe that you have accepted its invitation to the banquet of your life. A feast has been prepared for all who step beyond the familiar into the extraordinary.

Welcome home—your feast awaits!

KEY 1: YOU ARE THE POWER

STEP ONE:
"We admitted we were powerless over alcohol—
that our lives had become unmanageable."

KEY ONE:
"Through my conscious union with the Infinite Universal Presence, I am
powerful, clear and free. Through the realization that God is within me,
expressing as me, my life is in divine and perfect order."

Just In Time

I hung around Cocaine Anonymous (CA) and AA meetings for two years before I was even able to string ninety consecutive days together. As I look back now, I didn't actually want to heal at a deep core level. I just wanted to stop doing drugs so I could get my man back, and keep a job for longer than a month—maybe even get my daughter back. So I hung around the meetings, flirting and looking for approval with my dingy red dress on and a mouth full of cavities. I had barely looked at the 12 Steps hanging on the wall, let alone tried to practice them.

But over time, I came into contact with people at CA and AA whose lives seemed to be working. They had a sense of personal security and power. And I wanted that for myself. I wanted to have a life that I could be proud of, a home for my child and a mate who respected me. Sometimes, we need a reason to get serious about our healing. My reason started with wanting simple things. That was enough to begin stringing a few days together, then a week, a month and more.

I was entirely unprepared when one evening after being clean for almost ninety days—going to work on time and paying some bills—that "thing" happened again. My mouth started watering, my gut was in knots like I had just taken a laxative (symptom of a drug addict in the midst of a craving), and my heart was palpitating. I was ravenous for just one more hit—one last party. My inner voice said, "Don't do it, Sweetie, you're doing so well—please don't do it." I knew that once I started—once the monster was out of the cage— no matter how badly I wanted to stop, the binge would not be over until it was done having its way with me. Maybe this time, it would finish me off once and for all.

Even as I tried talking myself out of it, I was already out the door. I didn't even take time to put on a pair of shoes, I noticed as I was hailing a taxi. The hunger hit me so suddenly, and took me over so completely, it was if I had become possessed— blinded utterly by the insatiable need for a hit of cocaine. I knew that where I ended up was entirely out of my control.

> *"The alcoholic/addict will absolutely be*
> *unable to stop with the unaided will."*
> —Bill Wilson

I hopped in a taxi to take me to the neighborhood where I could feed the monster raging in my gut, my head and my soul. I was shaking as I got into the cab. I couldn't wait to get there. "Dunsmere and Redondo," I told the driver. I was already paranoid, looking around, sitting low in the back seat just in case someone from AA spotted me.

We drove a few blocks and the driver pulled over and turned off the engine. "What the hell are you doing?" I thought to myself.

"Hurry up and get me to the 'hood, man."

The face of God turned around and looked deeply into my eyes. He said to me, "Young lady, don't do it. You're better than this. Don't kill yourself. God loves you. I love you."

In that instant, I knew if I persisted on my current path, that day would be my last. The grace of God was speaking through this cab driver, extending to me the branch of life. I could listen, turn around and go back home, or I could drive on to certain death. The monster raged at the cab driver and said to me, "Don't listen to him, he doesn't know what he's talking about! Come on—you'll just get one and then you'll be done." But the loving will of Spirit had won. I heard God speak to me, and for once, I was listening. With tears in his eyes, the cab driver turned the car around and took me back home.

I had escaped the demoralization of another drugged out day and, more importantly, what I believe would have been a violent death. I believe with all my soul that had I not listened to the voice of Spirit speaking through that driver, November 1, 1986, would have been my last day of life. As it turns out, it was the day of my rebirth as a sober woman.

I must admit that when I went back to my meetings, I felt a little ashamed that I had almost gotten loaded again, but also grateful that the hand of God had grabbed me just as I was about to step off the cliff.

I called a friend from the program and told her what had happened. Making that call was a clue that I was serious this time. I didn't allow the shame of what I had almost done make me hide in secret. I reached out and shared that I was entirely ready to do what was necessary to save my life.

My friend said, "Ester, you've never really given yourself to this program. You've never worked the steps. You're too busy seeing how short you can wear your skirts to the meetings and how many eyes are on you. You're not focused on your recovery. What's it gonna take, girl? What've you got to lose?" And I thought, "Nothing—I've got absolutely nothing to lose. I have nowhere else to go and no more tricks up my sleeve."

I'd come to the end of the road. I had surrendered.

This time, I didn't walk around the meetings more focused on socializing and getting attention from men than actually taking the steps off the wall and applying them to my life.

A guy from Denver, Joe Hawk, came to Los Angeles to conduct Big Book Studies, and I immediately signed up. In the first several meetings, we took the first step, reading the Doctor's opinion and Bill's Story, where it talks about addiction being based on a spiritual malady, mental obsession and physical allergy. As we read those chapters, we broke down every line, until Step One came alive for me. "I'm powerless over alcohol (drugs), and my life is unmanageable," were no longer words, but living, breathing truths down to my very bones.

The first step scared me straight for a while, but I was warned that fear could keep me sober only for so long. I was told that self-knowledge of the nature of my dis-ease would be helpful to staying clean in the beginning, but would take a back seat when I least expected it—if I didn't continue in the process.

"Bring it on," I said. "This time, I'm ready."

How It Works

In Step One, you are indeed powerless. You have tried to effort your way into wholeness over and over again, just to fail over and over again. It is at this point that you are demonstrating a misguided belief in a God outside yourself—a God that isn't available or friendly, and deems you to be unworthy. But you keep begging and hoping that one day there will be mercy and a reprieve from the torment of addiction—a reprieve from the repeated pattern of pain and suffering.

Believe it or not, this is a wonderful step. It is an important and necessary starting point on your spiritual journey. But you were never meant to pull over and park there. Step One was designed to create a state of surrender such that you would stop trying to save and change your life from a limited sense of power. It opens a way for you to connect to the real power—the one power—Spirit.

In Key One, you get to take God out of the sky, churches and books, and put Him back within your own heart. It's from this conscious union that you are restored to wholeness and can reclaim authority, dominion and mastery over your life. In this Key, you take a journey from what you now believe about Spirit and your oneness with It, to an actual realization of this oneness.

The Work

Set your intention by saying quietly to yourself or out loud:

> "I surrender. I put aside everything I think I know about God, myself, and my relationship to God. My heart is open to having a realization of who I am as an expression of Spirit. I am ready and available for a new experience."

Contemplate

The "omni-" nature of God.

Omni means "all" in Latin.

The "all" of God includes all-power (omnipotence), all-presence (omnipresence) and all-knowingness (omniscience).

When I was first introduced to the concept of *omni* as the nature of God, I was genuinely floored. I was raised to believe in a God up in the sky who looked like an old, judgmental man, and who somehow had the capacity to keep His eye on everyone in the universe at the same time.

I used to wonder about that as a kid. How was it possible that the creator could do so many things at one time? I even had the audacity to ask my father, who was a Baptist minister. The answer I got was along the lines of, "He knows all, so you'd better be good."

This answer scared me to death, because as far as the God I understood was concerned, I was never going to be good enough. But it didn't make sense to me either.

When I began studying metaphysical teachings many years ago, I had the realization that the word "God" cannot begin to encompass the meaning of something that's infinite.

It's a word that was created to support us in describing the indescribable to ourselves.

You know there are many names for God: Spirit, Universal Presence, Tao, Life, Holy Mother, Father, I Am, Yaweh, Jehovah, or just "Hey, You." Sometimes God is referred to as Him, Her or even It. The point is, you can call God whatever you want. The spiritual healing and recovery of your wholeness isn't about what you call God. It's about having an expanded understanding of Its divine nature and a realization of your oneness with It.

That nature is the all of an infinite power, everywhere present. By definition, a singular infinite power cannot have an opposite. This may be difficult for some people, but I want you to consider the idea that there is no "otherness." There's not God and something else—like the Devil. There's only God.

Omnipotent: It is all-powerful.

Most people associate God with the positive things in life. In a "dualistic" universe—divided between good and evil—it's not hard to think of God as good.

But metaphysically, it's deeper than that.

God's qualities are expansive and creative in nature: love, peace, joy, harmony, health, affluence, excellence, synergy, and all the adjectives describing good that you can think of. After all, God is an infinite power.

God isn't even capable of knowing fear, disharmony, lack, limitation, dishonesty, cruelty or sickness, because an omniscient, infinite power and presence cannot contradict its own nature—even in thought. God doesn't even know death, because Its divine nature is eternal life.

If this is true, then what is the source of the discord or dis-ease that you're experiencing in your life?

In my work, I have found that dis-ease and human tragedy are primarily the result of our own thinking and our own illusions. We are vital participants in the story of Life. Our thinking and our actions affect our experience, the people in our lives, and the world around us.

So does my misfortune really have anything to do with God? Or could it be related to something else?

Since God is the good encoded in all things and is the only Power there is, is it really possible for evil to be real, or does evil appear to be real due to our perception and beliefs in a power separate from God?

This isn't to say that bad things don't happen, but only to say that those bad things may not be divinely orchestrated. Remember, a tree can grow and prosper even in soil where a horrific human tragedy occurred.

Life is still life. God is still God.

Omniscient: It is all-knowing.

Spirit is transcendent knowledge and divine intelligence, meaning God knows all there ever was or is to know. How awesome is that? This presence and power knows all things. There is nothing It does not know. What God knew a billion years ago, It knows today, and what is ever going to be known is also known now.

This Presence knows the way when, to your five senses, there appears to be no way.

In scripture there is a verse that states, "Lean not on your own understanding." Human understanding is finite and limited. It is often based on false beliefs and fears. But when you can lean into that which knows all, divine ideas and transcendent knowledge can be revealed and expressed through you—as you.

Omnipresent: It is everywhere present.

Like a hologram that retains its completeness even when divided into parts, the wholeness of divine power is encoded in Its entirety into all things.

And "all things" includes each one of us.

You might be asking, "How can I be one with God?" Let me give you an example of how that works:

Imagine I have a block of mahogany wood. Out of that block of mahogany, I create a table, a lamp and a chair. Even though the table, lamp and chair are in different forms, the essence of each is still what? Mahogany.

Or another example:

You're standing in front of the vastness of the ocean. The ocean is comprised of minerals, salt and water. If you take a cup and scoop up some of the ocean water, the quantity of the water in the cup will be finite and much smaller than the vast ocean, but its quality—the minerals, salt and water—will be the same. The quality of the ocean water didn't get diluted or diminished just because you separated it from the larger whole.

I'm suggesting that the same is true with you. God is an invisible yet all-powerful, all-intelligent force that individualized Itself as you. The same principle that created the sun, moon and stars out of its perfection, harmony and order, recreated Itself as you.

Let's break it down: the very air you breathe is God; your lungs that are inhaling and exhaling oxygen are God; the nostrils and mouth that allow the air to pass to and from your body are also God; the trees that release the oxygen—you got it.

There is no location in the universe that is not fully expressing this presence and power, whether you realize it or not. As you become aware of your true identity, you will see that the person brushing her teeth in the morning is not the sum total of who you are. You are—uh-oh, here we go...all the beliefs you were raised with are about to be challenged...this can't be true...yup—God!

Journal

Omnipotent means "all powerful." It is a term I use for the Universal power that is in all things—including us. There is a power behind: life, nature, the sun, the movements of the planets and everything else in our known universe. What does "omnipotent" mean to you?

Can you see how there could be a singular power behind all of the different manifestations of energy that we can see, and maybe even those which we can't see?

How would you describe the all-power, the only power, the one power in your own life? What does it feel like, look like and sound like?

What if there's no Satan or evil power, because there's only one power? How would your life be different if you knew, felt, believed that there was only one power operating in your life, and that power was only good?

How do you feel about being "at one" with God? What does that bring up for you?

Affirmations: Key One

Through my conscious union with the Infinite Universal Presence, I am powerful, clear and free. Through the realization that God is within me, expressing as me, my life is in divine and perfect order.

God is omnipotent—all-powerful. God is omniscient—all-knowing. Spirit is omnipresent—everywhere. God is the reality of all things, individualized as me—my true identity.

Just as the waves are another way the ocean occurs in nature, I am another way that God is occurring. All the power, goodness and love of God is right where I am. I feel safe and loved in this awareness.

Action Steps

Say quietly or out loud to yourself: "I set aside everything I think I know about God, myself and everything that's concerning me right now, and instead cultivate an open mind, open to new experiences."

Create a quiet place and put aside a minimum of 20 minutes every day for this process of contemplation and journaling. This is a very sacred time because you're about to let old patterns of belief die away and allow new beliefs to be reborn in their place. Take this opportunity to really give yourself all the nurturing and quiet time for contemplation that you need. You're worth it. This is your time.

Set your intention to know the nature of reality. Allow what is real to be revealed to you—independent of your past beliefs and cultural prejudices. Be free to accept this new view of reality, no matter how foreign it may seem to you right now. Reassure yourself that the Universe is one of order, peace and love, and that you have a special place in it—a perfect place.

Reread, review and process the Contemplations.

- Don't forget to journal any new thoughts that occur to you.

- Repeat the Affirmations slowly. Breathe deeply. Repeat again. Abide in the quiet.

- Practice this lesson every day for seven days.

Closing Thoughts

I remember how difficult it was to pull God out of the sky and connect It to my own being. Conceiving of myself and God as one just felt foreign and hard to grasp. I know that you probably feel the same way right now. There are probably some of you who, like myself at first, don't even feel worthy of saying that you're one with God—or it feels blasphemous based on the beliefs you grew up with.

What supported me in this process was patience, practice and more patience. Anything that is new to our way of believing and being is going to take practice. I didn't give up on myself. I was willing to fight for my life, and that fight meant realizing my oneness with God, no matter what it took.

Fight for your life, beloved. This is the truth about you—that you are one with God. This awareness is the foundation that will support every area of your recovery and your life.

The awareness that God is right where you are, as you are, and understanding the true nature of God is all that is needed to live life fully, joyously and completely.

Meditative Quotes

"Fundamental to your experience of 'good' is the development of your concept of what God is. God is the source of and is all creation. Don't limit God in whom rests all possibilities."

—Willis Kinnear

KEY 2: RESTORED TO WHOLENESS

STEP TWO:
*"[We] came to believe that a power greater than
ourselves could restore us to sanity."*

KEY TWO:
"Through my conscious connection with the One Power, I reclaim my spiritual dominion and emotional balance. I am restored to my original nature of clarity, peace and wholeness. I am restored."

I Lost My Way—and Became Insane

I continued going to meetings almost every day. I was so afraid of getting loaded again, I could've just moved my bed into an AA meeting. I was fighting for my life, and my self-worth was non-existent.

From where I stand today, I know that self-worth is a byproduct of integrity, clarity, balance, harmony and peace. Well, folks, that just wasn't happening in my mental household at this point. I wasn't drinking and using drugs, but my addictive patterns were still my master when it came to the men in my life. If it wasn't a man, it was food; if it wasn't food, it was seeking approval, or addiction to the negative mental chatter in my head. Sometimes I had all of my obsessions going on at the same time.

Boy, was I a mess.

At this particular moment in my life, I was obsessed with Mark—my boyfriend at the time.

An obsession is a thought that occupies the mind constantly and exclusively, so obviously there was no room in my already cluttered world for my daughter. Just when I thought, "Oh goody, I'm sober, I have a job and my own apartment, I can really focus on impressing Mark and make him love me," my sister announced—out of the blue—that she was sending my daughter back home to live with me. I argued with her and begged for more time. She almost had to threaten me into taking her back. This was after my sister had taken custody of my daughter for two long years because I was deemed unfit to care for her prior to my sobriety.

Here I was, two years sober and still saying, "I'm not ready to be a mother yet." But ready or not, my daughter was coming home.

Initially, I was happy to see her. The love I felt for her was real, but selfishness and self-centeredness were just as powerful. How was I going to see Mark whenever I wanted to? I only had one bedroom. How would I sleep with him if my daughter was home?

My poor little girl thought she was going to be the center of my world when she came home—which was her rightful place. I would catch her looking at me out of the corner of my eye, and I could see such hunger and longing for my attention on her face. I would get angry with her for wanting more of me than I had to give. I was angry with her for making me feel that awful guilt in the pit of my gut, and I was angry because I knew she deserved so much more.

I knew I was an awful mother, but felt as powerless against the urge to chase after Mark as I had when I was chasing the next hit of cocaine.

So, I put my obsession for Mark first. It really wasn't an obsession for this particular person, as I found out later in my recovery. He was just the misdirected focus of a wounded soul.

I was hungry for love, and looking for it in all the wrong places, yet was blind to the love staring me right in the face through the eyes of my child.

There are lots of women that do this—put their relationships with a man before the security of their children—and I was one of them. Not because I didn't love my daughter, but because there was a wounded child within my own consciousness that was suffering from the dis-ease of unworthiness, abandonment and all the pain of my past.

I didn't want someone to need or depend on me. I wanted to need and depend on someone that could take care of me—someone that could feed the insatiable hunger for approval and love I constantly longed for. I would choose people who resisted the job I had assigned to them—begging, manipulating and guilt tripping them into my needy world—all while ignoring the actual needs of my child.

I was, to put it frankly, insane.

Bill Wilson states, "The alcoholic cannot differentiate the true from the false."

The alcoholic mind is an obsessed mind—unconscious, wounded, fearful—and yes, "insane." The definition of insanity is "a complete lack of reason or foresight," or "doing the same thing again and again, expecting different results."

The chains of anxiety and obsession held me in bondage just as surely as a maximum-security prison located in the farthest corners of the earth might, and I acted on those obsessions.

My days began with getting my daughter ready for school—which was painful because I'd be yelling, and she'd be crying, and I'd feel like crap for yelling, but couldn't stop. Add to that my frustration and fear because Mark didn't come over or call the night before, then going to work trying to pretend I was normal while making a thousand personal phone calls trying to find the object of my obsession, and dealing with the million voices running through my head.

Going to the grocery store was a feat all by itself. I'd have an anxiety attack just trying to make the decision about which foods to buy for my daughter's lunch—tuna or turkey. Small things would send me into a state of fearful paralysis.

Insanity is a lot of work.

But I was still sober and starting to wake up a little more each day. My growth was slow and arduous—a little like watching paint dry. But every prayer, every meeting, was incrementally and slowly awakening me to something real.

I would go to my 12 Step meetings and literally fall into the arms of my sponsor. I'd be so exhausted from trying to manage my own life from an insane perspective. I grasped Step Two with the desperation of one who had nothing to lose.

And I had absolutely nothing to lose.

I came to believe that I could be restored, and the more I believed, the more I showed up for my life.

Then something weird started happening to me.

There came a day when I didn't care if I heard from Mark. There were mornings when I didn't wake up screaming at my daughter, and I could actually read a document at work and understand what it meant, because there was only one voice in my head instead of a million.

"I glimpse it. I can't grasp it yet, but it's there. What's that—maybe a little sanity?"

How It Works

I use the word "hypnotism" quite a bit in my work. I always thought it meant having someone sit in front of you with a swinging trinket, saying stuff like, "Follow the trinket until you become very sleepy, and when I snap my fingers you will hate brownies."

In a way this is true, but it actually goes a lot deeper than that.

Hypnotism is described as a "sleep-like state" or "when someone's attention is absorbed completely" in what they see.

Addiction is like a hypnotic spell, with its own rules, patterns and obsessions. When that spell of chronic fear, doubt, worry and low self-worth is broken by practicing the principles outlined in this book, we have the opportunity to awaken to life's truth—which is love, peace, balance and well-being.

When that happens, we return to our natural state of wholeness and are restored to sanity.

It is an imperative part of your recovery process to acknowledge that your thinking and actions have been completely insane in light of the pain, drama and discord they have caused to yourself and others.

The Soul Recovery process reveals that it's possible to be "restored to sanity," because sanity or "right perspective" is your original nature—who you really were in the first place.

My experience would suggest that insanity was not something I was created or born with, but was a state of mind that I learned, remembered, practiced and then experienced in my life.

Joel Goldsmith, founder of the Infinite Way, tells us that we have been hypnotized by our cultural history into believing we are less than expressions of God. He suggests that this false belief causes us to lose perspective of reality—and therefore experience insanity.

The Work

Set your intention by saying quietly to yourself or out loud:

"I allow the love of God to wash over me. I believe, know and accept that as I am restored to my true identity in Spirit, I will be filled with peace, balance, order, love and harmony."

"My mind is an expression of God's mind: focused, peaceful, free and clear."

Contemplate

I have found that chaos and insanity are based on an erroneous belief in two powers: the power of good (somewhere up there) and the forces of evil (somewhere down there). We seem to identify more with the power of evil, while praying for the power of good to help us overcome it.

The One Power, which is extensively talked about in Key One, is a principle of order, clarity, harmony, peace, joy and love. It is the only power and there are no other powers to oppose it.

The One Power constantly broadcasts its own thoughts of empowerment and clarity. We can then experience those thoughts when we turn our attention to it.

Maybe you have bought into the belief that there is more than one power, and that the thoughts and beliefs based on separation from God are founded in reality. They are not. They are based on fear, doubt, insecurity, shame and unworthiness. In short, they are insane.

Journal

Ask yourself:

Are my actions usually based on thoughts of unworthiness, shame, doubt, resentment and fears of abandonment or rejection?

- When was the last time you acted from that place? Describe the experience. What was the result?

- Who would you be without your wounds and false beliefs?

- Who would you be if your actions were based on wholeness, oneness and love?

- Who would you be if you knew that you were enough, and that you have enough, for a complete and fulfilling life?

Affirmations: Key Two

Through my conscious connection with the One Power, I reclaim my spiritual dominion and emotional balance. I am restored to my original nature of clarity, peace and wholeness. I am restored.

My soul is restored, refreshed and renewed. My mind is established in divine and loving order, free of mental chatter and mindless distractions. I am restored to sanity.

All the broken pieces in my life are restored to wholeness. The appearance of disorder is returned to divine and perfect order. The crooked places in my mind are made straight, because my mind is the mind of God expressing through me. This is the truth of me. This has always been the truth of me. I now remember—I am now awake to who I really am as an expression of God.

Action Steps

Start a list in your journal detailing who you were before you became hypnotized by fear and negative thought patterns, e.g., beautiful, smart, humorous, light, clear, balanced, peaceful, loving, lovable, honest, reliable—you get the picture. Even if you can't remember a time when you were not living a fearful and lonely life, try to imagine what it would be like by seeing the highest possibility for yourself.

For example:
"Before I became hypnotized by negative beliefs and fears, I was fearless, free, loving, open-minded, generous, fun, ambitious, trusting, centered and clear.

I knew there was nothing I couldn't accomplish. I trusted others with an open heart. I felt a sense of well-being and love. I loved life. I loved myself completely and was excited about life."

Write a one-paragraph script from a place imagining emotional health, balance and wholeness. Write it as if it is already accomplished. The script should explore how you feel and what your life looks like now that you have been "restored to sanity." Feel the shift in your entire emotional vibration as you do this.

Here's an example:

"Today I woke up with such a sense of well-being. I feel healthy, vibrant and alive. I'm so excited about my day. My thoughts are positive, centered and peaceful, and as a result I've created a wonderful life. I'm going to work in an atmosphere that I love. I'm surrounded by colleagues that respect me, and I respect them. I am on such a creative high because I am filled with confidence, and my mind is clear and brilliant. Every area of my life is overflowing with great relationships, financial harmony, and physical and emotional well-being. My life is amazing!"

It feels good, doesn't it?

This is the frequency you are going to achieve. Naturally, your environment will need time to catch up. Just continue to practice—even in the face of no agreement from your environment. A healthy mind slowly compels a new reality into being.

Experience follows practice.

Closing Thoughts

I had obviously displayed a complete lack of reason or fore-sight through most of my life. How many times did I go to score drugs with my entire week's pay in my purse, thinking I would only "do one" this time, after proving over and over again that "one" was never enough? How many times did I allow my utilities to get disconnected because I'd spent the bill money on drugs, and then had the audacity to curse out the representative at the phone company for turning off my phone? How many times did I put myself and my daughter in danger, taking her on drug runs with me at 4 AM?

If your insanity was never about drugs and alcohol, where in your life did this lack of reasoning and foresight play out? Are there times when you returned to the same unhealthy, abusive relationship over and over again, to the same gambling, shopping or eating habit again and again? How about just the recycling of painful and negative emotions that are keeping you stuck in an unfulfilled life?

That, my friend, is insanity with a capital "I"—a complete lack of reason and foresight.

That lack of perspective and emotional balance didn't completely go away when I became sober, nor when I took the first step. Bill Wilson states in the Big Book, "There is a long road of reconstruction ahead." Well, I was a little miffed at that. I thought that by getting sober, I would become a little like Mother Teresa, full of kindness and serenity. I thought all of my problems would go away. But the "reconstruction" had only just begun.

And it has only just begun for you, too. Now that you're clean and sober (or even if you're only in the "willingness phase"), it's time to start dealing with your consciousness. Consciousness is the sum total of your subjective and objective beliefs, awareness, understanding and experiences.

My consciousness was a quagmire of fearful, confused and distorted thoughts that had created traumatic experiences. You can probably relate to that.

It is much like an onion. There is layer after layer of deep-seated beliefs, wounds, and perspectives that are there to be acknowledged and healed. As soon as you think you've healed a certain issue and you're all done, there's another layer to be healed. Frustrating and discouraging, I know, but it does get better and better...as you continue to do the work.

I can promise you from my experience, when the hypnotic spell is broken by practicing the spiritual principles outlined in this book, you will awaken to the truth of life. You will return to your original and natural state of balance, clarity and order.

You will be restored to sanity.

Meditative Quotes

"What thought can do, thought can undo."
—Ernest Holmes

"Just as a tragedy and comedy can be written using the same letters, so many varied events in this world can be realized by the same atoms as long as they take up different positions and describe different movements."
—Willis Kinnear

"This Power works like the soil; it receives the seed of your thought and at once begins to operate upon it. It will receive whatever you give to it and will create for you and throw back at you whatever you think into it."
—Ernest Holmes

KEY 3: COMPLETE SURRENDER

STEP THREE:
*"[We] made a decision to turn our will and our lives
over to the care of God as we understood Him."*

KEY THREE:
*"I turn my life over to the care of the God I understand, know and embody
as love, harmony, peace, health, prosperity and joy. I know that which I am
surrendering to, and I do so absolutely. Knowing that this Power is the very
essence of my being, I say with my whole heart and mind: Thy will be done."*

Surrender—All Heaven Breaks Loose

My mouth was a mess, a result of a life filled with self-neglect, feelings of unworthiness and low self-esteem. When I was a child, my father was just beginning to get my teeth fixed when he became ill and died, and taking me to the dentist or to the doctor just wasn't on my mother's to-do list. So there I was, twenty-six years old, one year sober, and my mouth looked like—well, you can just imagine.

I always had toothaches. I thought it was normal, and that everyone had toothaches that kept them up all night long. I didn't know that it just wasn't right to smile with your mouth full of holes. But I was being restored. I had turned my life over to God—that which is divine love, order and whole-ness—and God ordered me to the dentist. I awoke one night with a toothache that was so painful, my ears were ringing from a near overdose of aspirin.

That's when I met my dentist, Mila Gutgartz. She took x-rays and declared my mouth a danger zone, but there was hope. She made out a plan of action and asked about my insurance—treatment was going to cost ten thousand dollars. Well, I had just started my job and didn't think I'd be covered for that amount, or at the very least the deductible was going to wipe me out.

God's grace—the Power within us that is the "way out of seemingly no way"—took care of it. The plan of action Dr. Gutgartz outlined took eight root canals, a mouth full of caps and a year to complete.

I kept waiting for a bill that never came.

I went to her office every Monday for an entire year. Each time, I felt like someone had just taken a hammer to my face. It was one of the most painful, yet lovingly profound experi-ences of my life.

"The pain pushes until the vision pulls."
—Michael Bernard Beckwith

Mila would hold me while I cried. The tears would just roll down my face when she would insert needles into the roof of my mouth. Sometimes one needle wouldn't numb me and I'd have to have three or four just so she could start working. It was hell, but she was so much more than a dentist, and she walked me through the fire.

For that year, Mila was the mother I never had—she was love and compassion in action. This sculptor of love rocked and held me as she chiseled my mouth into order.

She saw the complete idea—she knew I'd land safely on the other side, even when I thought I couldn't take one more step.

One day a tooth became infected after a root canal procedure. I was at work and I started feeling a little pain. After about an hour, the entire right side of my face was throbbing and I couldn't open my eye. The pain radiated down my neck, so I called Mila for an emergency visit and left work.

I didn't have a car at the time, so I caught the bus. The pain was so intense that I wet my pants. There I sat on the RTD, crying in excruciating pain with pee running down my legs. "I turn my will and my life over to the care of God as I understand God," I repeated to myself. I was willing to go through the fire—and I did.

Mila took one look at the tooth and confirmed it was infected. She prescribed antibiotics and Darvon, a prescription pain medication right up there with Valium and Librium—a drug addict's dream. Now, we are generally cautioned in the anonymous programs not to take any mind-altering chemicals, no matter what. But hey, my friends at AA weren't the ones sitting on a bus with pee running down their legs.

I took the pain pill as soon as the prescription was filled and I felt the effects immediately. "Oh, God, please don't let me get loaded," was my silent prayer. I feared for my sobriety because the high was feeling too good—and way too familiar. "Am I going to be able to stop with Darvon—or is this setting me up to go out and feed the hungry beast that is always lurking—waiting for an opportunity to snatch me back into the 'incomprehensible demoralization of addiction'?"

Silent prayers raced through my mind: "I will never leave or forsake you." "I offer myself to thee." My sobriety and new life felt like they were balancing on a high beam and losing the fight with gravity. I kept praying: "Thy will be done... Oh, God, I'm dying—please help me. Thy kingdom come..."

I dumped the pills down the toilet. I prayed and rocked— rocked and prayed—took Tylenol and my antibiotics. Spirit rocked me to sleep. The next day I went back to Mila. She rocked me too, and together we got through the death, the labor and the birth. I was still sober, and at the end of that year, I had a ten-thousand-dollar smile.

How It Works

"Let go and let God." That's what I did during that year of being sculpted and molded by God personified as Mila Gut-gartz. I surrendered my will and came out on the other side. Letting go is the hardest thing I've ever done and sometimes it's still difficult for me.

Why?

Because letting go is a process that challenges the ego, the sole purpose of which is survival. Surrender flies in the face of the ego's purpose. So it's no surprise that the survival of our personality and our self-image feels challenged when we surrender to something unfamiliar. It is outside of the ego's control. So we create this back and forth movement: As we surrender, the ego reasserts its will—which I call "self-will"— in an effort to take control until it gets so beaten up, we're ready to surrender again.

Well, I've turned my will over to God and have taken it back at least a million times. However, I don't hang out in self-will as long as I used to and I don't get beat up nearly as bad. I trust my higher self more every day, but letting that Power take over completely takes time and practice.

Based on an old belief about God, you're probably terrified of the idea of surrender. I can certainly relate to that. You probably think that if you "let go and let God," you're not going to get what you want and that your life is going to be boring, limited and hard.

On the other hand, there may be some of you who believe that when you surrender to Spirit, everything is supposed to change and become perfect with graceful ease immediately, and that there won't be any more challenges to walk through.

I have found that both these modes of thinking are unrealistic and false.

Here's why:

First of all, from the perspective of an all-loving, all-wise and everywhere-present God whose only desire is to express the highest and best through you, complete surrender is the key to lavish, unlimited good expressing in your life. Real surrender itself is not painful. Genuine surrender is blissful.

It is our resistance to giving up control that's difficult.

I have found that this experience of difficulty is true only if you're still struggling with a withholding, judgmental and moody God. The fault lies with our concept of a limited and Santa Clause-like God—keeping a list and checking it twice.

*"We were made in the image and likeness of God and
have been trying to return the favor ever since."*
—Michael Bernard Beckwith

If you see God as an unloving, withholding and punishing personality, you quite naturally would be terrified to turn your life over to It. I mean, why would you? But what if you were surrendering to an infinite source of good that is encoded in every person and every object in the Universe and that is the source of all love and well-being? You would most likely surrender your will and life with a lot more ease and trust.

Secondly, unless we are prepared for the pain and process of growth, the prospect of surrender can be discouraging and knock us off course.

Change is—by nature—uncomfortable. When you alter your way of being, thinking and feeling in the world, trust me, you will be outside your comfort zone. And if you're reading this book, chances are that your comfort zone, though not pleasant, is a place of safety for you. So there will be discomfort and some pain as you stretch beyond your usual patterns. This is completely normal. Remember, if you simply do what is within the scope of your usual way of being in the world, you will continue to perpetuate your current experience—and nothing will change.

When I turned my life over to God, it meant that I was willing to die to the old and be re-birthed into something new and greater.

This process of "dying to the old" is extremely painful to the ego, because it involves releasing something the ego has identified with and been dependent on for so long.

The labor of birth or of being restored can be excruciating as we are being pulled (or dragged—your choice) through the birth canal into something amazing and beautiful.

Change hurts.

When the sculptor is taking the chisel to the stone to create his highest vision—if the stone had feelings—I'm sure it would say "ouch." So, as the Universe is restoring and rebirthing us into its highest vision—the vision of who we were created to be in the first place—"ouch." Yet even with the "ouch" factor, we are divinely supported in this process of letting go and letting God, because in surrendering our lives to Spirit, we become acutely aware that we are not alone and that our personal lives are unfolding within a larger pattern.

Bill Wilson states in the Big Book: "We make a decision that in this drama of life, God is our director. He is the principal, we are his agents. He is the father and we are his children."

I don't take his meaning to be "his children" in the context of separation, as in "he" is up in the sky and we are down here.

No, I mean that *you* are the microcosm of the macrocosm. Each of us—no matter what we have or haven't done—are individualized expressions of the One Power as explained in Key One.

This Power is love Itself. From a place of faith and absolute readiness, you surrender your life to this infinite vibration of unconditional love, and behold as you are made new.

The Work

Set your intention by saying quietly to yourself or out loud:

> "I offer myself to that which created me in its image and likeness. I surrender my life to the love and adoration of Spirit. The entire Universe is conspiring for my highest good, joy, harmony, order and wholeness."

"I fearlessly and joyously surrender my life to Spirit within, knowing It only desires the very best for me. With absolute abandon, I say with my whole heart and mind: Thy will be done."

Contemplate

Spirit loves Itself as me—completely, fully and absolutely.

I am willing to understand, believe and know that Spirit would do anything to support my health, happiness and well-being.

Suggestion: Just *feel* into the above ideas. These contemplations might seem especially abstract because you can't quite receive that kind of love yet—so just take your time and start by imagining it first. There's no rush.

"I am willing to know and feel that God is bursting with pride when I am fulfilled, happy and successful, because that fulfills God's mission. Spirit wants this for me because It wants to express as me. It is God's pleasure to support me in all ways."

How does that feel?

Spirit is constantly and personally interested in you, It is individualized as you and is ever available to you—because It is you.

Journal

Ask yourself: Is God separate and apart from me, or is Spirit within me—as me—is me?

Can I see parts of myself that are pure and powerful?

44

Suggestion: Really take your time here. Maybe you believe you've made so many bad choices, there's nothing good about you. Not true. Find something—anything—that's wonderful about you. Start small. If you try, you'll find the diamond in yourself even among the rough places.

- Can I trust a loving God enough to completely surrender to It? If the answer is no, why not? If yes, why?

- What is it that you fear in total surrender? What do you believe will happen to you if you do?

- If you are able to surrender, can you feel the weight leave your body in the places where you've been holding on to your self-will instead of God's will?

- What are you feeling right now in your surrender? If you're still feeling fear, go back and read the beginning of Key Three.

Affirmations: Key Three

I turn my life over to the care of the God I understand, know and embody as love, harmony, peace, health, prosperity and joy. I know that which I am surrendering to, and I do so absolutely. Knowing that this Power is the very essence of my being, I say with my whole heart and mind: Thy will be done.

The nature of God is Love, forgiveness, harmony, prosperity, health, fulfillment, creativity, kindness, clarity,

peace, faith, confidence and wholeness. This is the power
I turn my will and life over to.

Action Steps

Think of a person who was once in your life or who is currently in your life that made you feel unconditionally loved
and supported. Maybe it was your mother or father, a grand-
parent, aunt, uncle or teacher. This individual just adored you
and was there for you, no matter what. They would do anything to support your vision, success, health, happiness and
fulfillment.

They love you—completely and totally.

If there was no such person in your life, I want you to
think of a person that you love in that way. If you can't think
of someone that way, then simply try to imagine what it would
mean and what it would feel like to be loved that deeply and
powerfully.

Now, I want you to multiply that feeling by a hundred,
two hundred, a thousand. Feel the awesomeness of being
loved and accepted so unconditionally—just sit with that for
a moment.

That is a fraction of how much you are loved and adored
by the Universal Presence—Spirit, God, whatever name you
are most comfortable with.

Think of every aspect of your life: your beliefs, health,
finances, relationships, concerns, resentments and desires.
Take the smallest concern to the greatest one—from the
mailman delivering your mail on time, to the results of the lab
work you've just had done at the doctor's office.

Take them all one by one and offer them to this Presence that is only love. Give your life, piece by piece, to this Power that deems you worthy of all the good there is.

Say quietly to yourself or out loud this prayer of surrender:

"God is all there is. It is omnipotent, omniscient and omnipresent. This power and presence is only good and only love. God is individualized as me. It is where I am, what I am and who I am. From this place of oneness, I free-fall into this presence of divine order, love, peace and harmony. I offer every aspect of my life to that which created me out of Itself. In complete faith, I let go and allow the fullness of Life to have its way with me. All is well and perfect.

"I am grateful. And so it is. Amen."

Closing Thoughts

I remember a time in my life when "Thy will be done" meant a life of drudgery, boredom, scarcity, sacrifice and all the attendant experiences that came along with releasing control. In practicing the Keys, however, I not only had a revelation, but the deep spiritual experience that God's will was better than anything I could have imagined or created for myself. Just like you, I was skeptical at first, but scripture invites us to: "Prove Me now herewith, if I will not open the windows of heaven and pour you out a blessing that there is not enough room to receive" (Malachi 3:10).

Spirit has proven itself to me, over and over again. So now I release much more readily and easily, knowing that in doing so, something wonderful is about to happen.

My desire for you is that you relax and trust that all is well, now that you have taken this courageous step of free-falling into this all-loving, all-powerful presence within your own heart. You are in the best hands you have ever been in. As we anchor in the awareness of the unlimited power of love, we can say with our whole hearts and minds, "Thy will be done."

Meditative Quotes

"'For I know the plans I have for you,' declares the LORD, 'plans to prosper you and not to harm you, plans to give you hope and a future.'"
—Jeremiah 29:11

"I will restore to you the years that the locusts have eaten."
—Joel 2:25

"Behold, I make all things new."
—Revelations 21:5

"Father, I offer myself to thee, to build with me and to do with me as you will."
—Third Step Prayer, AA Big Book

KEY 4: AN EXAMINED LIFE

KEY FOUR:
*"Through my absolute surrender and conscious connection to the One
Power and Presence, I courageously, deeply and gently search within myself
for all thought patterns and behaviors that are out of alignment with love,
integrity, harmony and order."*

What's Your Story?

I was so resentful of Mark—remember him? This is the same
guy who was out sleeping with another woman while I sat
on his front porch at 3 AM waiting for him to come home;
the guy I once went to jail for after defending myself from
his physical abuse; the guy I made my daughter sleep on the
couch for, while he slept in the bed with me; the one who constantly cheated on me. Yup, I was pretty pissed off at him and
all the other Marks I had totally given my power to.

I thought all men were dogs, and I thought I was only
worthy of men that were dogs—so guess what type of men I
kept attracting in my life?

No mystery there.

I was so angry at my sister, who wouldn't allow me to spend the night at her house prior to my sobriety because she had the audacity to think I would steal from her (I would have)—but I was absolutely appalled. This is my sister, after all.

The blame, hate and resentment I felt towards my mother was lodged solidly in my heart. I resented her for not wanting or loving me, for abusing me emotionally and physically, and for treating me as if the sole purpose of my existence was to be an object for her mistreatment. As far as I was concerned, she was the cause of all my shame, feelings of unworthiness, of being unloved and unwanted. It was all her fault, and I was going to make her pay by hating her for as long as I could.

I resented my father, who adored me but would not stand up to my mother when she was beating the crap out of me or embarrassing me in front of my friends. Then I felt guilty for resenting the only parent who ever showed me love.

I was resentful of my daughter for being born while I was still a child myself. I wanted to have sex at sixteen years old, not get pregnant for God's sake. But at sixteen that's what I was: pregnant, seventy-five pounds overweight, abandoned by my baby's father, constantly running away from home to wander the streets in the unforgiving summer heat of New York.

I blamed her for my guilt because I couldn't be a good mother. I blamed her because I was expected to be a mother before I was ready. I blamed her for forcing me to look at how screwed up I was.

Did I mentioned terrified? Yeah, I was terrified.

On and on it went. I was mad at the world, for the world had not treated me fairly. Everybody was wrong—except me.

I thought for years that if I didn't have the mother I had, I wouldn't have been so screwed up. If I had boyfriends that were true and honest, I'd have felt loved. If I hadn't gotten pregnant at sixteen, I'd get to do what I wanted to do, when I wanted to do it. These mental chains held me in a self-imposed prison until I decided to set myself free through forgiveness and taking responsibility for the part I played in my own life.

Turning my will and entire life over to the care of a loving, all-powerful God gave me the courage to look at all this debris hanging out in my head, heart and soul. I felt an immediate shift as soon as I began writing my "victim story" about how people had screwed me over. I was blown away when I realized that my ego (the part of myself fighting for its survival) had made others accountable for my well-being. Writing it down transferred the garbage that was weighing me down out of my head and onto the paper where I could see it more clearly.

In order to see things the way they really were, I had to develop a willingness to face the truth and a level of honesty I didn't even know I possessed.

I was willing—finally.

I found out that I was a very wounded and frightened young lady—and I had acted out of those wounds and fears most of my life. I realized that I wasn't totally blameless for how messed up my life had become. I saw the part I played, knowingly or unknowingly, in a lot of situations. I saw how my belief in my own victimhood allowed me to stay a victim.

It wasn't easy to do this work. I wanted to keep hating my mother and blaming the men in my life for the way things had turned out. Blame was something I was used to. It was a familiar feeling.

I used blame as a lens through which I related to the world. It allowed me to be right, by holding onto my memories of the very real—and not so real—injustices that were perpetrated upon me. I'm not saying that people who abused me acted appropriately in any way. But there were times when I either placed myself in a position to be hurt, I held onto the hurt, or I felt like a victim because of another's need to take care of themselves instead of taking care of me. Blame allowed me to avoid looking at issues that I did actually have some control over—issues that I was just not ready to address yet.

But holding onto blame and resentment did not get me a better life.

Releasing it did.

How It Works

There is truth for us all in Bill Wilson's quote from the Big Book: "For alcoholics, resentment is the number one offender. It destroys more alcoholics than anything else."

Key Four is where you set out on a course of vigorous action by doing a deep, thorough "resentment-forgiveness" process.

Resentment is the remembering, re-telling and re-living of a painful event, even when the event is securely in the past. If you're honest with yourself, the blame, stories and resentments you're currently holding onto may have happened yesterday, twenty years ago, maybe even longer—yet you're still re-living them.

How can you tell when you're still living in resentment? The person you have a story about is not allowed safe passage through your awareness when you think of them. Your body does an involuntary jig, where you have sort of a clenching sensation in your gut when you think of the circumstances associated with that person. No matter how much you tell yourself you have forgiven, your spirit can't embody the lie, and it reacts in your body when you think of that person or situation that caused you pain.

Why is it so difficult to release resentment? I believe it's because you cannot forgive the effect until you've healed the cause. The cause of your pain is not "out there." It's within your own core beliefs and wounded perceptions, which then get projected onto others. Those "others" then mirror back to you the false beliefs you hold about yourself.

For example, there isn't anyone out there who can "push your buttons" if there aren't any buttons already there to be pushed. Those buttons—what I call "core wounds"—are feelings of abandonment, rejection, shame, unworthiness, betrayal, etc. Yet you most likely believe that the reason you feel hurt is because of something someone did to you. The truth of the matter is, the core wounds (or buttons) were already there—operating as your dominant way of thinking about yourself. The people you resent just happen to be the perfect vibrational match to those core wounds. It should not come as a surprise that they are now featured in the role you subconsciously assigned them to play, with all the drama and pain showing up on the stage of your life.

You've essentially created a "victim story" about the painful circumstance, which you cultivate, remember, re-tell and re-live over and over again. The path to your freedom lies through forgiveness, because it is the only way you can reclaim your power. But until you heal the underlying core wounds, move beyond the old story and create a new and empowering narrative—real forgiveness is just not possible.

So it's vital to take the power out of the victim story you made up. Colin Tipping shared a great story about that: "The Navajo Indians had a ceremony for doing this. Anyone with a grievance could come to the circle three times to tell their story, and they would be heard. On the fourth occasion everyone would turn their backs. 'Enough already! Your story is just a story. There's no real truth to it—it is just an illusion. We have heard it three times and we no longer wish to give it power. Let it go and then let yourself move towards what is really true.'"

In turning your life over to God as you did in Key Three, you become willing to do things that you would not and could not ordinarily do—like take a microscopically honest, "fearless moral inventory" of all the beliefs, feelings, resentments and actions of the past and present. Your core state of mind doesn't disappear because you've turned your life over to God. Surrendering to God actually puts you in position to go deeper in your inquiry than you ever dared venture before.

It is impossible to maintain the spiritual connection made in Key Three when you are filled with resentment, fear, selfishness and self-centeredness.

I've come to believe that the reason for this is that the vibrational frequency of Spirit is operating at a higher, purer rate than the frequency of resentment and blame.

It isn't that the Universe has changed its mind, or is no longer interested in you when you can't connect to it. It simply cannot lower its vibration to meet you in a frequency of resentment.

Every belief and feeling you have is operating at the vibrational frequency of your dominant thought patterns. Your experience is not based purely on your words or your wants, but is primarily based on your emotional vibration. I'm sure you've noticed that the words people use to communicate are often less important than the emotional vibration they are "thinking and speaking from." This is an example of how frequency of thought operates in the human dimension.

In the spiritual dimension, God is naturally operating at the highest rate possible, beyond what we can ever imagine. You can consider this to be like a TV station or channel that is constantly broadcasting love, peace, joy and ecstasy. When we are tuned in to this station, we have tuned in to our true identity and our experience reflects this as feelings of absolute joy, freedom and peace. It feels amazing when we're tapped into that frequency because joy, freedom and peace is our true nature in spite of all the mental pollution that may be broadcasting on other "TV channels" as resentment, blame and fear.

You can tell when you're tuned in to a negative channel, because you're pissed off, miserable and full of fear. You could even suffer from physical exhaustion because the frequency of that channel acts as weights upon your body, mind and soul, causing feelings of hopelessness, depression and ill health. This is why it is so important to heal core wounds, transform your story from victimhood to wholeness, and release blaming your state-of-being on anything or anyone—including yourself. You must forgive in order to be in alignment with your highest good—or your highest vibration.

Spirit cannot and will not contradict its own nature to meet you in a state of victimhood, so we must raise our vibration by tuning in to the highest frequency we can find in order to meet the fullness of the Divine Presence.

That is the work that Key Four is designed to address.

The Work

Set your intention and say quietly to yourself or out loud:

"I claim spiritual dominion, courage and authority as I go deeper than ever before. I examine my life, thought patterns and behaviors in a vibration of safety and love. My freedom is more important than being stuck in self-righteous pain."

"I am open and willing to discovering those parts of myself that no longer serve me. I release the stories that have held me in bondage, and am willing to see the truth that sets me free."

Contemplate

Staying attached to my story keeps me stuck in my pain; releasing my story heals the pain.

My core beliefs (core wounds) of unworthiness, shame, abandonment, rejection, etc., will continuously mirror back to me as people and circumstances until they are healed.

Forgiveness does not condone inappropriate behavior, it transcends and protects me from inappropriate behavior because I am now operating from a higher spiritual level.

I don't have to like the person I am forgiving, but forgiveness frees me from my attachment to the story surrounding that person—one way or the other.

Journal

Do you blame others for the circumstances in your life? If so, where has that gotten you?

Does telling your story over and over again about the painful situation make you feel empowered or disempowered?

Are you ready to release the old story and create a stronger, more loving and empowering one? If the answer is no—why not?

How far are you willing to go for your freedom?

Is your life based on making all or most of your decisions from a wounded and fearful state of mind? If so, what are the results of making decisions from that place? Do you get what you really want or do you get the limited version of what you think you deserve?

How do you feel about taking a fearless and moral inventory? Does it frighten or excite you?

What do you hope to experience in this process of becoming more aware of your resentments and moving towards forgiveness?

Affirmations: Key Four

Through my absolute surrender and conscious connection to the One Power and Presence, I courageously, deeply and gently search within myself for all thought patterns and behaviors that are out of alignment with love, integrity, harmony and order.

"Get ready, my soul—I'm diving in."
—Daniel Nahmod

Action Steps

Allow for at least 20 minutes per day for this process. For your most challenging issues, it may take up to an hour. Take the time, because this is one of the most important processes in your work.

First, you need to prepare for this process by having 3 sheets of—ideally—unlined paper. You will be placing the paper horizontally (long way across) so that you have enough room. If you happen to have "ledger" (11" x 17") or "legal" (8.5" x 14") size paper, that's even better.

On the first sheet, create three columns labeled "Resentment," "My Story" and "I Believe." Make sure you leave more room for the My Story and I Believe columns.

On another sheet of paper, you're going to create an additional two columns for "My Contribution" and "Core Wounds" sections, and on the third piece of paper, make a column for "Repeated Pattern."

Fill in each section with the following information:

1. *Resentment:* The person, situation or institution that you have an ongoing grudge against.

Remember, resentment is the remembering, re-living and re-telling of a painful event long after that event has passed.

Write the name of the person, circumstance or institution that you resent.

2. *My Story:* Your perception of what is happening in the present or has happened in the past regarding the person, circumstance or institution you have resentment against.

Yes, it is okay to list under resentments any anger you have towards yourself and God.

Write your story version of what happened (no more than two or three sentences).

3. *I Believe*: This section is where we look deeply into our belief system—what they are, where they came from and how they express as beliefs we have bought into. Remember, our ego—whose prime directive is survival—has generated beliefs to support our survival.

There are seven parts of our ego that can be affected when we experience resentment. They are:

- *Pride*—What I believe others think of me.

- *Self-Esteem*—What I believe about myself.

- *Security*—What I believe I need, but am not getting.

- *Ambition*—What I believe I want, but am not getting.

- *Sexual Relationship*—I believe this situation is a threat to my sexual relationships.

- *Personal Relationships*—I believe this situation is a threat to my personal relationships.

- *Financial Security*—I believe this situation is a threat to my financial security.

Write out your belief system using the seven points of belief outlined above.

4. *My Contribution*: The part you played in this particular situation, i.e., your own beliefs, actions and patterns of behavior that contributed to the disharmony of this relationship or situation.

- *Selfish*: Did you only think of your wants and needs, and not the wants and needs of the other person? Were you willing to only see things from your perspective, and not the other person's perspective? Did you want someone to change to make you feel comfortable, secure and validated?

- *Dishonest*: Were you dishonest by omission or commission? Did you say yes when you meant no? Did you remain quiet when you had the opportunity to speak up? Did you delude yourself that this person was your source and security?

- *Self-seeking*: Did you bad-mouth this person to others in order to make him or her look like "the bad guy" and you look like the victim?

- *Afraid*: Were you afraid of not getting what you thought you needed? Afraid of what others thought of you? Afraid of being excluded? Afraid of being abandoned and rejected or alone? Afraid of financial insecurity? Write out how you contributed to the situation.

5. *Core Wounds*: Core Wounds are dominant thoughts and beliefs we have about ourselves, and we usually blame others for being the cause of those wounds. The wounds usually fall under the following categories: Abandonment, rejection, shame, insecurity, unworthiness, powerlessness, betrayal, confusion,

humiliation, abuse or—more generally—feeling unloved, unwanted, powerless, used, small, invisible, damaged, dirty, etc.

Write the core wound or wounds that caused you to respond in the way that you did.

6. *Patterns*: Patterns are repeated thoughts, beliefs and behaviors that show up time and time again in various situations in your life.

List three or four areas or relationships where these patterns are showing up in your life.

Process Example

1. *Resentment*: Musical Director

2. *My Story*: He didn't pick me to sing the lead vocal part, because I'm not famous and he's a jerk.

3. *I Believe*:

- *Pride*—Affects my pride because I believe he thinks I can't sing, that I'm not good enough.

- *Self-Esteem*—Affects my self-esteem because I don't believe I'm good enough.

- *Security*—Affects my security because I believe I need his approval to feel worthy and good enough.

- *Ambition*—Affects my ambition because I want him to think that I'm good enough, and I want to believe that I'm good enough.

- *Personal Relationships*—Affects my personal relationships because I believe he doesn't like me, and I feel uncomfortable around him because I feel ashamed and unworthy.

- *Sexual Relationships*—Does not apply in this case.

- *Financial Security*—It affects my financial security because I believe if he doesn't think I'm good enough, he won't hire me again or he'll give me a bad recommendation to other musical directors and I'll be out of work and won't have enough money to live on.

4. *My Contribution*:

- *Selfish*: Only thinking of my wants and needs to be chosen and validated, and not his need to have the right person for the part. I only saw this situation from my perspective of rejection and not-enoughness, versus his perspective that he needed the right person for the part.

- *Dishonest*: Made up a story about what he was thinking based on my own false beliefs about myself. He never actually told me I wasn't good enough. Deluded myself that I needed his validation in order to feel capable and worthy. I was dishonest by omission because when he asked me what was wrong, I said "nothing" instead of sharing my feelings.

- *Self-seeking*: I talked about him to the other singers to make him look like the bad guy, and to get validation from them that my feelings were correct. Tried to alter their opinion about him so that I would feel better about myself.

- *Afraid*: I was afraid that he thought I wasn't good enough; I was afraid that I wasn't good enough; I was afraid of being fired; I was afraid of getting a bad recommendation to other musical directors and no one would ever want to hire me; I was afraid of looking bad; I was afraid that I was a loser.

5. *Core Wounds*: I felt rejected, judged, unworthy, not good enough, unaccepted, excluded, small, abandoned and afraid (of financial insecurity).

6. *Patterns*: When I'm around other mothers, I feel unworthy, small, shamed, judged, damaged; when I'm around other singers I feel afraid, unworthy, judged, rejected; when I'm in a relationship with men I feel abandoned, rejected, unloved.

Do you see how this fits together? Each issue we have energy around should get this treatment. This purpose of the Key Four process is to take those issues out of our head, away from our emotional chatter, and place them on paper so we can see these beliefs, contributions, core wounds and life patterns more clearly. This clarity is a vital first step to resolving these unresolved issues from the inside out.

Closing Thoughts

I used to joke that I must have an invisible banner stuck to my forehead that read, "All really screwed up, emotionally unavailable guys please come be my man," because that's all I seemed to attract. It took quite some time to realize that—based on my core beliefs and wounds—I actually did have an invisible banner written across my forehead!

I remember one emotionally abusive relationship I was involved in, where I was ready to flee—again. I told my spiritual advisor—"I'm out of here." The pain was so intense, and my wounded inner child was in a constant state of feeling rejected, abandoned and really frightened. My advisor's response was shocking. She said "Ester, you don't get to leave this time with the same set of beliefs that drew this relationship to you in the first place—you must stay and do the inner work that will heal your wounds and change your old story." That's exactly what I did. So, instead of fleeing the relationship, I practiced the exercises in this Key, lifting my vibrational frequency such that it was no longer possible to stay in a situation birthed in neediness, unworthiness and pain—and I transitioned with love and grace out of the relationship.

My unhealthy thought patterns—from the space of a wounded belief system—mirrored back to me as negative experiences in the form of people and circumstances. Why? Because what I constantly thought about, dreamed about, talked about and believed, had to express in my outer world. When those unhealthy patterns began to heal through the process of forgiveness, I began to attract positive experiences in the form of people and circumstances.

"It is done unto you as you believe."
—Matthew 9:29

The people who seemed to have hurt you the most are also operating out of their own false belief system, core wounds and stories. It's not your responsibility to worry about them, or even try and fix them. Through your own process of forgiveness, you will tap into an energy of compassion and understanding for others. It is from that place of clarity, self-forgiveness, forgiveness of others and compassion, that you will make a choice based on the highest good for all concerned—whether to stay in a relationship (the relationship may vary from friendships, jobs, relatives, etc.) or allow it to fall away with your freedom, dignity and peace of mind intact.

Forgiveness has literally given me back my life. It is my hope that when you commit to the work outlined in this Key, you will also experience a radical shift in your spiritual practice and mental attitude. From there, the possibilities are endless.

Meditative Quotes

"Selfishness and self-centeredness—that, we think, is the root of our troubles. Driven by a hundred forms of fear, self-delusion, self-seeking and self-pity, we step on the toes of our fellows and they retaliate. Sometimes they hurt us, seemingly without provocation, but we invariably find that at some time in the past we have made decisions based on self which later placed us in a position to be hurt."
—Bill Wilson

"What opens the circle to someone's heart to allow more than just their answer?"
—Anonymous

KEY 5: LIVING OUT LOUD

STEP FIVE:
*"[We] admitted to God, to ourselves and another
human being the exact nature of our wrongs."*

KEY FIVE:
*"I claim the courage and willingness to share the exact nature of my mistakes
with another spiritual being. I am heard with compassion, unconditional love
and wisdom. In this loving vibration, clarity, peace and balance are restored."*

I Have a Secret

I pocketed my pride and was willing to spill the beans on myself. I found an angel in an Alcoholics Anonymous meeting. Her name was Treva, and she was the most beautiful woman I'd ever seen. She became my sponsor and turned out to be the perfect expression of Spirit to guide me to the next level on my spiritual path. Treva had practiced spiritual principles in her own life—she walked her talk, and I wanted what she had.

I told her everything—and I mean everything.

I sat before her with a secret that had been burning in my soul about me and my cousin June Bug, ever since I was twelve years old. I was shaking with shame and fear that she would judge me, and maybe even throw me out of her house.

But I told her anyway.

June Bug came to live with my family when his mother died giving birth to his sibling, and his father was a chronic alcoholic who could not care for him. He wet the bed all the time, and when I think of that five-room house we lived in, the smell of urine always accompanies the memory. We used to pick on June Bug, and thought it was very funny that he wet the bed. He was either being laughed at or getting into trouble, which in those days meant he was getting "a whuppin'." He wasn't very good looking, and he was shy and kind of hunched over. He had big eyes, and one eye sort of turned in.

June Bug was a good target for abuse.

I had no compassion for him. He was just June Bug, my ugly cousin who wet the bed. He wasn't really a part of my family—he was a charity case. I treated him the way I was taught to treat him by the rest of my family, and of course treating him badly made me feel better about myself.

I remember at four years old, my immediate family was assembled to take a family picture. In the room where we were photographed, there was a mirror on the side of the wall. Years later when I looked at the family photo, there in the mirror was the reflection of June Bug, sitting off by himself. Not a part of us. Not good enough to stand with us and be in the family picture.

As I got older, my parents became even more rigid and strict. The kids in my family were only allowed to go to school, church and the front yard. There were no play dates with neighbors or friends. No extra-curricular activities. So, at eleven or twelve years old, June Bug became my extra-curricular activity. I was curious about sex, but of course could

Rogers Family Photograph circa 1965. Includes: nephew Eugene, brothers Michael and Bobby, mother Esterlee, brother Leeroy, father Buck Vernon Rogers, sisters Maerita and Liz. Ester and niece Helen are in front. June Bug is reflected in mirror - far left.

never talk about this with my minister father and very religious but abusive mother.

June Bug was sixteen. I, in my desperation and feelings of isolation, loneliness and curiosity, pursued and molested him. When I tired of the game, I told my father that he had molested me. June Bug was ridiculed, humiliated, roughed up and thrown out of the house.

My entire family blamed it all on June Bug and shunned him for the rest of his life.

When it came time to do my fifth step in recovery, this story hit me like a ton of bricks; I had totally blocked it out of my mind. But here it was, the harm I had caused to someone totally innocent of any wrong-doing.

June Bug suffered for how he was treated by me, my family, and of course the choices he made in his own life. In his early adulthood, he was found homeless and dead under a bridge.

When I finished telling my story to Treva, it was like a 2,000-pound weight had been lifted from my shoulders, but I was afraid to look her in the eye. I still feared I would find judgment and disgust there. But when I lifted my gaze to meet hers, I saw and felt only unconditional love, compassion and forgiveness. A huge layer of shame had been lifted from my heart, and I was beginning to sense the truth of my divine birthright: freedom.

How It Works

Secrets keep us sick. They keep us in shame and uncertainty. Secrets lead us to think we are the only ones who have ever had dark thoughts and shameful experiences. They keep us separate and apart from the world, from ourselves and from the possibility of having the spiritual connection we long for. When our guard is down, and the mask that we show to the world slips for an instant, we are ashamed that we have been exposed for who we appear to be, until we are willing to be transparent and honest with someone who can support us in seeing ourselves for who we truly are.

We are not our mistakes, nor are we our past actions that are out of alignment with our essential nature.

Our out-of-balance actions are ALWAYS manifestations of a distorted view of ourselves and those around us. From that place, we have committed many sins against ourselves and others. We have not sinned based on the Christian theology of being denied God's grace—which is impossible in the realm of an immutable, all-loving principle.

Instead, we have sinned by missing the mark of order, harmony, peace and love.

John Ringland says, "The word 'sin,' metaphysically speaking, is associated with illusion and delusion, which causes us to get out of sync with the harmony of the cosmic symphony. This, then, gives rise to acts that are out of harmony with the whole and create dysfunction and suffering."

So, in Key Five we connect with someone who has a conscious understanding of the emotional and spiritual housecleaning we have committed to. We share this with someone who understands how we committed certain acts of "sin"— not because we were bad people, but because we were diseased people at the level of our emotional make-up, and we experienced a false sense of separation from God.

Ideally, this should be someone who has gone through the same process. No one can understand you better than a person who has walked in your shoes.

The Work
Set your intention by quietly saying to yourself or out loud:

> "I surrender my false sense of pride, and allow it to be transmuted into unconditional love and safety. I surrender to the loving nature of Spirit within. I am safe as I share every secret that has caused me shame and produced feelings of unworthiness. I am ready to share every secret that has caused me to hide. What was in the dark now comes to the light. I am ready to hold my head up high, and look the world in the eye as a free, empowered expression of God."

> "The love of God embraces all of me—even parts that I am still learning to accept about myself."

Contemplate

In sharing my secrets with an understanding, spiritually awake person, I am making myself available for the unconditional love of God and other people. I am opening the door to freedom.

My secrets have made me feel isolated from others, and I am now ready and willing to know my oneness with all of life by no longer hiding.

Secrets keep me guarded and block me from my good and my joy.

I am not my mistakes nor am I my actions. My out-of-balance actions are manifestations of a distorted view of God, myself and those around me.

In sharing my secrets in the loving, wise presence of another, I am released from the bondage of self and set free to live out loud, and to live fully.

Journal

What have you been hiding? What is your secret?

How does it make you feel to put your secrets down on paper?

How do you feel about the idea of sharing your deepest, darkest secrets with another? Are you afraid, embarrassed or ashamed?

Are you willing to trust God and the person you have chosen to share your secret with—and know that you are safe and loved?

If not, say the affirmations from Key Three and those in the next section until you are. Move through the fear and do it anyway. All is well.

Who are you when you are free from secrets and shame?

Example: Free, calm, confident, compassionate, approachable, unguarded, forgiving, loving, emotionally available, peaceful, empowered, generous

Affirmations: Key Five

I claim the courage and willingness to share the exact nature of my mistakes with another spiritual being. I am heard with compassion, unconditional love and wisdom. In this loving vibration, clarity, peace and balance is restored.

This journey home is a long and winding road, but I will not get lost. I am led, guided and loved every step of the way.

Action Steps

Set an appointment with someone this week to share your secrets with. You want this to be someone you respect as a person of understanding and integrity—someone you feel safe with.

This person could be a spiritually-minded friend, mentor or minister—but you want this person to be someone who is willing to see the part of you that is bigger than your history, your problems or your issues. There are many available communities that can assist you towards finding this person. These include AA groups, spiritual communities and more.

Author's note: I have had many people contact me directly to find a good spiritual advisor, and have assembled an ever-growing list of qualified coaches and therapists who can assist you through the various processes assembled here. Please see the "Resources and References" section at the end of this book for more information.

Closing Thoughts

I never wanted anyone to know how insecure I was or that I was racked with jealousy when someone else was experiencing a good that I desired. I never wanted anyone to know that I had debased myself for drugs or that I put relationships with men over the welfare of my daughter.

And I never wanted ANYONE to know about June Bug.

Yet revealing those dark feelings in the presence of love shed a light on every nook and cranny of my consciousness that had been running my life—those secrets which had been pushed way, way down in my subconscious mind.

I support you as you do the same.

You are not a bad person, no matter what you have done. You just forgot who you were as a whole, perfect and complete expression of God. The purpose of Soul Recovery is to remind you of just that. This process is going to wake you up and restore you to sanity, peace, self-love and the magnificent person you were created to be.

The person you choose to share your secrets with will have the capacity to listen lovingly and objectively—and be able to see things from a higher perspective. They will see things that maybe you can't see right now.

My own process was extremely humbling, yet oh-so-liberating. I had to admit the things I had done in my past and own up to some of the twisted thoughts that I continued to harbor and which I still reckon with today.

Yes, even me, with so many years of sobriety and all the spiritual work I've done—even I still have work to do. The job is never fully complete, but gets easier and easier as you sincerely and consistently do this work.

Key Five is a vital step on the road to self-realization because without uncovering and revealing our secrets, we tend to retreat right back into the delusional parts of our story that created the issues in the first place.

We need each other on this path. You don't ever have to walk alone. You have angels on earth and beyond who are supporting you, willing to love, support and champion you through this revitalizing process.

Meditative Quotes

"Where two or more are gathered in my name, there I am in the midst."
—Matthew 18:20

"It's vital to be growing through your life rather than going through your life. The object is not to change other people or situations; it's to do the inner work they stimulate."
—Wally Amos

"Once we have taken this step, we are delighted. We can look the world in the eye. We can be alone at perfect peace and ease. Our fears fall from us. We begin to feel the nearness of our Creator. We may have had certain spiritual beliefs, but now we begin to have a spiritual experience."
—Bill Wilson

KEY 6: HONORING THE INNER CHILD

Key Six:
"I am now ready to release all thought patterns and behaviors unlike my true nature, which is wholeness. I free-fall into the loving presence of Spirit within, and allow it to heal every known and unknown false belief. I am transformed by the renewal of my mind."

The Forgotten One

I had been sober for several years since that day of sharing my darkest secret, and had learned a lot in my sobriety. Yet as much as I had learned about God, and had even experienced the power and love of God, I still had a hard time accepting that I was worthy of the blessings that came into my life.

Where did these feelings of unworthiness come from, and why did they feel so real and so deep? I was frustrated at knowing what I knew about God, doing the work I had done, yet still feeling afraid of my own shadow. This shadow of the past would show up right in the midst of something great happening to me. I didn't understand what was going on until I went way back into my childhood, to the times and places where I believe my "mental chains" were created.

A Memory . . .

The trees in the backyard are my adoring fans, the broom is my microphone and I'm singing at the top of my lungs. I love music and it loves me back. It never abandons, rejects or abuses me. Music is my safety, and I give it my heart.

I'm in fourth grade, and so excited to be singing for the first time in front of a live audience. I don't care about my mother who acts like she hates me, or the kids who tease me and don't want to be my friend.

When I'm onstage, the lights, the music, the audience make me high and nobody can touch me—that is, until the night of my first concert at Parkside Elementary School.

When I was getting dressed to go to my concert, I couldn't find my blue skirt and white blouse—the uniform required for chorus members. It wasn't hanging in the closet, but then again, no clothes were hanging in my closet. They were on the floor, where all my clothes were, wrinkled, dirty and mixed in with the clean ones. Well, I just had to go to my concert. I picked through the dirty clothes, frantic and terrified that I wouldn't find what I needed, and then they wouldn't allow me to sing. Singing was all I had—I had to go. There, in what seemed like a ton of dirty clothes, was my blue skirt and white blouse. The button on the skirt was missing, so I got a big safety pin and pinned it together. My white blouse was dingy, stained and wrinkled, but it would have to do.

A big responsibility for a nine-year-old, but the diva was going to her concert—no matter what!

My older sisters arrived to take me to the concert, but before they could see how I was dressed, I put on my big coat to cover up. I knew if they saw the wrinkled, dirty blouse and pinned up filthy skirt, they wouldn't let me go. My little heart knew that I wasn't presentable, but my warrior Spirit was damn sure gonna try. So, off we went.

When we arrived at the school, we were directed to the cafeteria where the other children in the chorus were getting lined up to enter the auditorium. They looked great in their crisp white tops and freshly ironed blue bottoms. When my sister told me to give her my coat, I knew the moment of truth had arrived, but was hoping that my wrinkled, ripped and dirty attire would somehow go unnoticed. I very slowly unbuttoned my coat and stood exposed in all my ragged glory. My sisters took one look at me and said, "Ester, you cannot go onstage like that."

The world stopped. I begged, I pleaded, I fell on the floor, I did pushups. "Pleeeese, I beg, don't do this to me." I was simply wailing while a river poured from my heart through my eyes. They dragged me out of the cafeteria in what felt like slow motion. I was humiliated in front of about two hundred kids, who were saying, "What's the matter with Ester? Why is she leaving? Bye-bye, Ester."

It felt as if—at nine years old—my only reason for living had just been ripped from my very being. Not to speak of the embarrassment and shame I experienced.

When my sisters got me to the car, I opened the back door and literally collapsed into the back seat. My heart was bleeding, and I felt like nothing would ever be okay ever again. When we arrived home, I ran into the house, searching for the only sanctuary I had, my father. I passed my mother in the hallway, who was looking at me as if I'd done something wrong—instead of having the bright idea that maybe she should've washed and mended my clothes to prepare me for my concert. What a concept.

I fell into my father's arms, which were opened and waiting for me before I even reached his office, because he heard me howling from the depths of my being the moment I entered the house.

The pain and humiliation I experienced that night became etched deep in my awareness as the lie that I wasn't enough, and disappointment was a way of life.

I was wounded, and only a deep embodiment of God's love and my oneness with that love could heal me.

And it does.

How It Works

I know you're probably thinking, "I've already surrendered in Key Three"—and that is true—but it's important to know how complex we are as developed personalities. We resemble a web of issues, beliefs and wounds that are still operating in our lives, and we are in a constant process of unraveling those threads. After all, as I quoted earlier, "there's a long road of reconstruction ahead."

Key Three gave you the power and courage to move forward. Key Six takes you into a deeper understanding of your history and yourself, with the humility to allow Spirit to heal yet another layer of your wounds and beliefs.

Step Six states, "We were ready to have God remove these defects of character."

"Defect," as defined in the dictionary, is "a failing, blemish, or flaw, especially one that still allows the affected thing to function, however imperfectly; or a personal failing, weakness, or shortcoming, especially in character."

I refer to these defects as "core wounds and beliefs" that replay and recycle in our consciousness and experiences over and over again—until they are healed.

I know that there are those of you who have done a ton of spiritual work, but seem to get stuck in the same areas over and over again. You're not alone—there are many of us that have done that as well. As referenced in Key Four, you have taken on a set of false beliefs and stories as the truth of your identity and, because it is "done unto you as you believe," your experience mirrors back to you these very thoughts and beliefs that you've embodied, practiced and released into the Universe.

Key Six is inviting you to go deeper as you revisit your childhood and explore what happened to you in highly specific terms. You're not revisiting your past from a place of being a victim, but rather from a place of understanding what's really going on under the surface—what's driving your thoughts and actions. It is from this understanding that you will recognize the past-generated beliefs creating your experience that are no longer serving you.

To "become entirely ready to have God remove our distorted, wounded ways of thinking" are more than lofty words. Entirely means ENTIRELY. You need to be willing to surrender every single belief, thought and behavior that is out of alignment with your worthiness, your deservingness of all good, and your wholeness.

The Work

Since we experience what we believe at a core level, we want to take a deep and honest look at the stories and wounds that keep the painful and destructive patterns showing up in our lives, over and over again.

Like the Big Book, I say that the fullness of Spirit is woven into the fabric of your very being, but in order to fully know and experience the truth of this, you must surrender the illusions about yourself that you have taken on as your identity and be willing to have that which no longer serves the good of anyone removed.

Set your intention by quietly saying to yourself or out loud:

"My past no longer has any power over me. I release the deep-rooted false beliefs of unworthiness and shame, and in the awareness of my oneness with God, all of the ways I have walked in pain dissolve into the nothingness from which they came."

"I am whole, perfect and complete. I am loved, adored and cherished by the entire Universe. My past was an experience, not my identity. My identity is God in expression."

"I embrace my inner child in a vibration of unconditional love, acceptance and forgiveness. I am willing to love my inner child more than he/she has ever been loved."

"I release and I let go. I let the Spirit run my life."
—Rickie Byars Beckwith

Contemplate

The past is not my fault, and I release the shame, blame and pain of my childhood.

My childhood was a reflection of how I saw myself. I forgot that I was enough, wonderful and amazing.

How I see myself can be changed through prayer, meditation and self-forgiveness.

I was never damaged, unworthy or stupid. I am created in the image and likeness of beauty, intelligence, order, balance and all the magnificence of the Universe. I am now waking up to this truth. I am awake.

Journal

What was it that happened in your childhood that made you believe you weren't enough, or that you were unlovable, unwanted, damaged and unworthy? Was there one main event that caused it, or were there lots of different events that established this pattern in your life?

Important Note: I just want you to write a page about this experience, like in the My Story section of this chapter. I don't want you to live in the story for too long. We do not want to build our mental house there. Our work here is to just get an idea of what created the false belief system in the first place.

How are these thought patterns and behaviors showing up in your life now (finances, relationships, career, addictions, family, etc.)?

Example: As you know from the story that opened this chapter, I had bought in to the belief that I could never be good enough to do what I loved, which was sing. Every time I was put in a position to sing, my insides would quake with fear, my breath would become shallow and my notes would come out flat or sharp. My belief about myself was reflected in my musical performance and would come to life every chance it got.

These thought patterns are perceptions of an inner wounded child. What is your child saying to you when he/she feels threatened? Ashamed? Guilty? Not enough?

What does your inner child say to you when something amazing is happening in your life—when something you really wanted has finally shown up? Can you accept it, or do you sabotage the good?

Finally, are you willing to let Spirit heal you (your inner child) and completely remove the blocks you've set up in your life?

Affirmations: Key Six

I am now ready to release all thought patterns and behaviors unlike my true nature, which is wholeness. I free-fall into the loving presence of Spirit within, and allow it to heal every known and unknown false belief. I am transformed by the renewal of my mind.

By acknowledging and embracing the pain and shame of my inner child, I am entirely ready to allow Spirit within to heal and restore me to wholeness.

Action Steps

Practice seeing yourself free from the false beliefs developed in your childhood. What does your life look and feel like without them? Practice by writing a paragraph in your journal.

Example: I am free and confident. I joyfully show up for my life knowing that I'm enough, and what I have to offer is valuable and worthy. I move through challenges, knowing that I am divinely supported by a friendly Universe and that Life is for me—and that nothing is against me. I live from a space of knowing that God is conspiring for my success, my fulfillment and my good.

From your healthy, awake and conscious adult self, I want you to rewrite your childhood by imagining how you would lovingly support, want, adore and protect your inner child. I want you to do this every day, by looking at one or two of those painful circumstances and think about how you would have taken care of your child if you were the parent that is conscious and awake. This is an opportunity to "re-parent" yourself by giving your inner child the love, respect, safety and acknowledgement that he/she deserves. Only you can do this, because your actual parents could not see the whole picture in the same way as you can see right now.

Here's an example: As a loving, spiritually awake adult, I wash, mend and iron my inner child's clothes for her concert. I lovingly bathe her, fix her hair and dress her for her first concert. I am so proud of her, and can't wait to see her in her debut performance feeling secure, loved, protected, supported and prepared. I am sitting in the audience just beaming at her. She looks out and sees me sitting there with my heart overflowing with love for her. She knows she is loved. After the concert, I take her out to celebrate with any treat she wants. When we get home, I bathe her again in a fun bubble bath, washing her back and going over every moment of the concert with her, just gushing about how proud I am of her. Then I lovingly tuck her into bed, kissing her on the forehead and watch her fall asleep. She rests in the love of God as my love. She knows she is safe and adored.

When my inner child is feeling afraid, I will comfort her with loving words, prayer and meditation. I'll ask her what's going on, and what does she need? I will listen to my inner child, be understanding yet firm in my awareness that God is love, and that I am enough. I will do my spiritual work until my inner child feels safe and protected in every area of my life.

Closing Thoughts

I've come to the realization that alcoholism and addiction didn't just happen to me. I wasn't born a cocaine addict. I don't believe that I was born with addictive genes or an addictive personality. I believe I was born under the illusion of separation from Spirit, and that my addictions were simply the effect of that illusion.

Addictions don't just happen and I wasn't born with them, but I do believe that I was born "into" them. I was born into a vibrational frequency of pain, fear, and ignorance, because the world I was born into had forgotten its own identity of wholeness, and I took it on.

I believe that I subconsciously chose all of my experiences from that illusion. So even when I was clean from drugs and alcohol, I was still spiritually asleep to my wholeness.

My addictions were created from one core belief building upon another until I was convinced that my fears, resentments, shame, guilt and negative experiences were reality.

If you've had similar experiences, you have been operating under that illusion as well.

Key Six was the most difficult one for me because I couldn't understand how it was possible that I could be such an expert at what I knew about God, with so much recovery under my belt, and still be so screwed up.

But in revisiting my childhood, I experienced a new understanding of the many layers of pain that were operating in my subconscious mind—even after so many years of recovery. From this understanding, it became easier to have compassion for myself and develop a new sensitivity for my inner child.

This might be one of the most difficult keys for you, too, because in addition to the many layers of healing involved, there are some behaviors that you still may get some "benefit" from: negatively berating yourself, overeating, smoking, gambling, addictive sex, gossiping, etc. Even though the consequences of these behaviors are often harmful, and sometimes even deadly for yourself and others, it's your hell and you're used to it.

Just know that these patterns of behavior are survival mechanisms your inner child has set up to protect you. As strange as it may seem, at different points of your life those mechanisms probably served and protected you. But as you go deeper into your recovery-restoration process, I promise you will come to know that you no longer need this kind of protection and that it is actually impeding your recovery.

As you release these behaviors by doing the work, you will come to realize that you are always completely safe in the loving, infinite arms of Divine Intelligence!

Meditative Quotes

"The wound is the place where the light enters you."
—Rumi

"... and I ask you right here please to agree with me that a scar is never ugly. That is what the scar makers want us to think. But you and I, we must make an agreement to defy them. We must see all scars as beauty. Okay? This will be our secret. Because take it from me, a scar does not form on the dying. A scar means, I survived."
—Chris Cleave, *Little Bee*

"Be ye transformed by the renewing of your mind."
—Romans 12:2

KEY 7: NEVER GIVE UP

STEP SEVEN:
"[We] humbly asked Him to remove our shortcomings."

KEY SEVEN:
"In loving compassion for every aspect of my being, I humbly surrender to the love of Spirit. I know myself as a perfect expression of Life. I surrender all, and I am restored to the life I am created to live."

Spirit Says to Sing Your Song

I didn't open my mouth to sing for the first ten years of my sobriety. I had totally shut that part of my life down. For ten years, I was so afraid of not being perfect, I wouldn't even allow myself to sing in the shower.

But something was happening to me.

I was slowly waking up to the gift I had been born with. I started to remember that I loved, loved, loved to sing—and even my fear and feelings of unworthiness couldn't keep the gift and desire hidden any longer.

I remember sitting in the car with my sponsor, Treva, and saying to her seemingly out of the blue, "I want to sing." She simply responded, "Well then sing, baby."

I started to shyly test the waters in the shower, then hum a little in front of my daughter—who was very encouraging and supportive. Then I joined a band that some guys from AA had put together. I sounded like crap, like a bird that hadn't flown in a very, very long time. They kind of sounded like crap, too—but it was fun and we were a good match.

Then I found myself sitting in the congregation at Agape International Spiritual Center, a huge metaphysical church in Los Angeles. I was there for the message and to continue my spiritual growth.

Well, be careful what you ask for.

Everybody was on their feet singing the congregational song, "I Release and I Let Go," and I found myself on my feet singing it too, when all of a sudden the choir director, Rickie Byars Beckwith, looked over to me and mouthed the words "I want to talk to you." I pointed my finger back at myself, mouthing "me?" and she nodded, yes—you!

After church service ended, I went to see what Rickie wanted. She told me she had heard my voice above all the other voices in the audience (what's the chance of that happening?) and that there was a solo part she wanted me to sing on a new song she had just written for the choir. My heart was racing with excitement, gratitude and absolute terror at this amazing opportunity.

She gave me a tape of the new song to practice and learn by Wednesday night choir rehearsal—a mere three days away. I was so scared, thinking, "She really doesn't know that I'm not very good, and now she's going to find out on Wednesday night."

I practiced, prayed and practiced some more. My voice was cracking, weak and a little off key (even I could hear that). I didn't know what I was going to do, so what I did was humbly offer my frightened inner child, the part of me that was so afraid of being exposed in all her ragged glory, to Spirit. I surrendered the fear and insecurity I was experiencing to a power that was greater than myself, but was—in fact—my true self.

I arrived at rehearsal and Rickie introduced me to the choir. I was shaking with nervousness and my throat felt like it had closed up. But my desire to live my passion was bigger than my fear, and I was willing to fall flat on my face in order to live the life of my dreams.

And flat on my face I went. My biggest fear had come to fruition. I didn't sound or look good that night, not because I wasn't enough, but because deep down inside I still believed that I wasn't enough. But there was something within me that knew better than that, and refused to give up.

And Rickie saw and heard something in me as well. She kept giving me opportunities to sing until my wings became stronger. She believed in me until I started to believe—a little at a time—that my dream wasn't a childish fantasy, but was very real.

I can't count the times I got up to sing at church and sounded like the rough had never quite gotten out of the diamond. But I wasn't going to give up, no matter how humiliated I felt, no matter how many times I thought I had failed—and no matter how many of those "looks" I got from other singers who weren't having the issues I was having.

I wasn't going to give up.

You see, my soul knew that the little girl who used to sing to the trees with the broom as her microphone had to sing her song. So as much as my little wounded child wanted to hide, Spirit had outed me—and there was no turning back.

In a demonstration that there are no accidents in God, the two songs I had soloed on were called "God's Unchanging Grace" and "Spirit Says to Sing Your Song."

God's grace has indeed been my sufficiency ever since.

How It Works

Humility is the willingness to know your oneness with love—even when you can't feel it.

Humility is saying: I have no clue how the Universe is going to change and heal me, but I know that I can't do it for myself. Unless and until I sincerely, humbly and willingly give Spirit everything, my life is going to continue to be full of drama, crap, half-starts and half-completions, and I will be blocked from living the life of my dreams.

Key Six guided you toward becoming entirely ready to have God heal and transform every wound, belief and thought pattern that continues to block you from the good you're seeking. Key Seven will take you deeper into surrender and allow the Universe to prove to you that it's got your back.

You have done amazing work up until this point—so don't stop now. Though it may be tentative, you are probably starting to step out on what sometimes feels like shaky faith. Or you have proven to yourself—by practicing the other Keys—that Spirit is there to lead you when you least expect it.

The previous Keys have prepared your heart and mind to surrender your fears, insecurities and false beliefs. They have supported you in getting more clarity about your past conditioning, thoughts and behaviors that have been blocking you from the best life you can have.

Key Seven is about taking actions that are in alignment with this new willingness to surrender.

For example:

- You are willing to surrender addiction to all substances.

- You are willing to surrender compulsive overeating.

- You are willing to surrender your fear of letting go.

- You are willing to surrender blame and judgment of yourself and others.

- You are willing to surrender the need to be right and the destructive habits of getting into personal relationships from a place of need and unworthiness.

- You are willing to surrender the habit of sabotaging the good that you desire.

- You are ready and willing to surrender past stories and experiences that have dictated your sense of deservingness and self-worth as expressed in Key Four.

- Surrendering doesn't just mean praying a prayer and affirming positive words. It means that you're going to actually cooperate with the prayer and affirmations by taking positive action.

- When you couple sincere intention with divine action, you cannot and will not fail.

The Work

Set your intention by saying quietly to yourself or out loud:

> "My old thoughts and behaviors are not the boss of me. The almighty Universal Presence and Power that resides within my very being is the boss of me. Spirit is governing my life because it *is* my life. I can't do it alone and I know I can't do it alone, but there is an almighty, omnipotent presence that can, and is—even now—renewing my mind and my life."

Contemplate

In offering all parts of myself to God—the places of myself I am aware of and the places I am not aware of—and walking in the direction of my soul's true desires, I am healed.

Even though the road of reconstruction is long, I am on my perfect journey. Everything is unfolding in my life—on time and in perfect time.

I revisit the dreams of my childhood—before I forgot who I was—and through complete surrender of my shortcomings, the years that have been lost are given back to me.

Journal

As a result of the work you have done so far, have you come to a place where you understand that your problems are not "out there," but are mirrors of your own emotional/mental make-up and spiritual disconnection? If not, what are your thoughts about the challenges in your life?

Can you see how your early childhood conditioning "taught" you how to be insane, afraid, delusional, but you were created as an amazing, perfect and complete person? Explain.

Are you ready to stop allowing your destructive, fearful beliefs from running your life?

If not, why not?

If so, how?

Can you believe now that you were created in the image and likeness of a perfect, loving, friendly and unlimited God? Explain.

What does it feel like to experience total liberation from your old story and negative beliefs?

Example: It feels scary to step into my new identity. Even though I was miserable before, at least my misery was familiar. Though I'm afraid, I'm also excited by the possibilities awaiting me. I feel like something new and wonderful is happening to me.

What dreams have you buried that you are now ready to bring back into the light?

Write a two-paragraph script of how your dream is unfolding in your life—from a place of freedom, confidence and self-love.

Example: My website is finally completed. It's so beautifully and professionally done. I'm receiving lots of product orders, calls and bookings as a result of my website. I wake up every morning feeling energized, excited and ready to begin my day. I've never felt this strong and positive before. I love the changes that have happened in my heart, mind and soul. I am so excited as I watch amazing things happen in my life.

Affirmations: Key Seven

In loving compassion for every aspect of my being, I humbly surrender to the love of Spirit. I know myself as a perfect expression of Life. I surrender all, and I am restored to the life I am created to live.

I humbly surrender my entire being to the love of Spirit. I am supported by the entire Universe as I surrender to the grace of God that is always my sufficiency, and am guided to perfect and right action.

I am walking my talk and taking action in direction of my dreams. As I faithfully move in the direction of my heart's desire in thought, words and action, I am supported by the entire Universe and my dreams come true.

Action Steps

Each area of your life that has been revealed as a product or result of old wounds, beliefs and behaviors, is now calling for new action on your part.

Fold a piece of paper in half. On the left side, list the top three issues you are currently dealing with. On the opposite side of the page, write positive actions steps you are willing to take that are in alignment with your healing (*see sample chart on the following page*).

And for God's sake, if you want to sing—start singing!

CURRENT ISSUE	POSITIVE ACTION STEPS
Finances out of order; owe money	Start paying off debts (even if it's at a rate of $2/week) Balance checkbook and commit to keeping it balanced Stop spending money I don't have Start a savings account, even if I can only contribute a small amount every month
Addiction to sex and relationships	Commit to Anonymous meetings Find a sponsor, spiritual guide or therapist Find a church in alignment with my new beliefs, to ground me in a community of like-minded thinkers Ask for help Continue to abstain from dating for six months to a year, and totally devote time to my healing
Procrastination of Life's Dreams	Get clear about my dream Research on internet about how to get started on my dream Talk to friends about my dream Commit to acquiring the tools I will need to make my dream a reality. If I dream of dancing, I will start taking dance lessons. If I dream of being an entrepreneur, I will read books on business and try to take a class at a local community college. If I want to be an author, I will start writing for 10 minutes every single day.

Closing Thoughts

I can't tell you how many times I've had the opportunity to sing, and was so frightened of failure that I thought I would pass out; or the numerous times I opened my mouth to sing and a flat note came out. I'd be so humiliated, I'd find myself behind a 24-hour mini mart at 2 AM with donut glaze dripping down my chin.

I can't tell you how many times I found myself in debt to others with my checking account overdrawn, or the many times I've arrived in the same pattern of unhealthy relationships with men—expecting different results.

Key Seven directed me to give all my childhood wounds and beliefs up to an immutable, loving and ever-present power that gave me the strength to show up for the life I had dreamed about since I was a little girl. It gave me the clarity and power to be alone and to focus on myself instead of looking for yet another relationship from the same wounded perspective. It gave me integrity about my money issues and the courage to change my patterns about finances.

Was making those changes comfortable? Absolutely not. I was shaking in my boots most of the time, but once I got sober, I showed up for my life no matter what it took. The desire for living life to the fullest had more power than my fear and discomfort.

It's now time for you to show up for your life in a big way, not just by talking the talk, but by walking the walk. Yet at the same time, be patient, loving and merciful with yourself. Remember, these core wounds and habits have been operating for a very, very long time. It's going to take a commitment to prayer, humility and surrender to convince your inner child that he/she is safe, loved, deserving and worthy of good.

We never have to convince God of this fact, but sometimes it takes everything we have to convince ourselves that it's normal and right to have a wonderful and fulfilling life.

Meditative Quotes

"If you want to have something you've never had before, you're going to have to do something you've never done before."
—Dr. Barbara King

"For my thoughts are not your thoughts, neither are your ways my ways, sayeth the LORD. For as the heavens are higher than the earth, so are my ways higher than your ways, and my thoughts than your thoughts."
—Isaiah 55:9

"I surrender all of myself to the God within to transform and restore me, because I can of mine own self do nothing."
—John 5:30

"Whatever you can do, or dream you can do, begin it. Boldness has genius, power, and magic in it. Begin it now."
—Goethe

KEY 8: WILLINGNESS

STEP EIGHT:
*"[We] made a list of all persons we had harmed and
became willing to make amends to them all."*

KEY EIGHT:
*"I acknowledge the people I have offended based on false beliefs, fear, doubt
and unworthiness. I am willing to go to any lengths to clean up my side of
the street."*

Facing the Music

Resentment woke me up one morning. It felt like a wasps' nest had exploded in my head. I was so pissed off at just about everybody in my life.

I was angry at my daughter, who just wouldn't heal and get on with life the way I wanted her to. I kept trying to convince her that my opinion about her life was the only one that mattered, but she wasn't buying it.

Big surprise.

I was angry at my ex-boyfriend for not loving me the way I couldn't seem to love myself. The voices in my head were trying to create the perfect way of convincing him that he needed therapy so he could be healthy enough to make me happy.

I had a disagreement with two of my best friends about a song we'd written. As far as I was concerned, I was totally right, but they just wouldn't see it my way. I was afraid of hurting their feelings and I was afraid of getting the short end of the deal.

Then there was my brother, who absolutely adores me and the feeling is mutual, but every time we got together, he had this passive-aggressive way of showing his jealousy. We'd be in the middle of a conversation, and all of a sudden, he'd want to sing a song to see who could hit the highest note.

Oh yeah, I was mad.

All of this was going through my head, and to top it all off, I lost my eye glasses. They're not the reading kind that you just put on to read small print. I'm talking the bifocal kind, the "prevent walking into walls" kind. And I couldn't find them anywhere. I looked under the couch, in the freezer, in the microwave and under the mattress of my bed. They simply disappeared.

I was filled with resentment and fear, *and* I couldn't see anything.

I stopped in the middle of the madness and called my spiritual advisor because it was clear I was off center, and I didn't need to talk to someone that would agree with my drama. I needed someone who loves me enough to tell me the truth, and I knew just the person.

Gary said, "Make a list of all the people you are resentful at and become willing to clean up your side of the street.

When you clean up your side of the street, you'll find your freedom."

"Are you kidding?" I thought to myself. I didn't want to even think of cleaning things up with people who had cheated, betrayed, lied to and hurt me. Oh, hell no . . . I'd rather die than do that. Forget that madness. Some things are better left unsaid. Let the dead bury the dead. Leave the past where it belongs—or better yet, let them apologize to me, for once.

That was my attitude. And my prison.

My friend and advisor asked me, "Ester, do you want to be right or do you want to be free?"

Well, when I considered shelling out another three hundred dollars for a new pair of glasses, and burying my emotional pain with Krispy Kreme donuts until my tongue was numb and my stomach was so bloated it would hang down to my knees—freedom started to look like an easy choice.

I prayed for the willingness to do what was necessary to set myself free. June Bug was at the top of my list. My daughter was running a close second. Even my mother—who I felt had caused me the most harm—made it on the list.

I was afraid that the people who had blatantly caused me harm were going to think I was a doormat or a wimp if I sought to make amends to them first. They might even have the audacity to think they were right to have treated me the way they had.

In the end, I realized it was none of my business what they thought—my only business was my side of the street.

Even as I started writing names down on the list, I could feel the guilt, shame and blame begin to fall away. The energy

I had devoted to not taking responsibility for my actions and blaming others immediately started to flow.

I even found my glasses! They fell out from the blankets at the foot of my bed, where I had spent hours looking the day before.

The good I desired had been there all the time.

Where I was blind, now I see.

How It Works

Key Eight requires that you make a list of people you have knowingly or unknowingly harmed. You might think, "Well, if I've unknowingly harmed them, how will I know to put them on my list?" You'll know because even if you unknowingly harmed someone—meaning you're not sure exactly what you did to cause hurt—you will feel a tense and uncomfortable energy in their presence. Anyone you feel some negative energy with or who you're hesitant to be around belongs on your list. Putting them on your list shifts your energy from victim to freedom, and from blaming others to looking squarely at your own contribution to an unhealthy situation.

Key Eight takes the people we have harmed knowingly or unknowingly out of our subconscious, puts them onto a piece of paper, and brings them out into the sunlight of the Spirit, where healing happens.

Just this act alone starts the ball rolling.

I realized during this process that I had harmed myself just as much as I had harmed others. So I put my name on the list right along with the other people I was going to make amends to. Jesus the Christ said, "As you have done unto the least of these, so have you done unto me" (Matthew 25:40).

Meaning that what I've done to others, I did to myself—because we are all one.

That's why when we betray or dishonor someone, we feel sick inside. The feelings that accompany our wrongdoings are guilt, shame and unworthiness. By becoming willing to make amends to others allows us to become willing to forgive ourselves. We understand that we acted in certain ways—not because we were bad people—but because we were insane, broken, wounded people that did bad things. From that place we begin to look at ourselves, our pasts and others with deep compassion and understanding.

For instance, I was a horrible mother.

Yes—I was.

There are times when I remember how I treated my daughter and cringe with shame and disbelief that I would treat any child that way.

But after practicing this Key, I now understand that I was an underdeveloped, broken, wounded, cocaine-addicted seventeen-year-old child, who simply could not give what I didn't have.

So no matter how you've judged yourself or have been judged, your past actions were motivated by the pain of your own limitations. It doesn't make it right, but it does make it understandable.

You can't give what you don't have. And if you knew better, you would've done better.

Having compassion for yourself does not let you off the hook for past wrongdoings. In fact, it makes you more accountable. Acknowledging and accepting that accountability makes the work of this Key a whole lot easier.

When we commit to this Key, we are signaling to the universe: "I'm willing to do ANYTHING to wake up to my wholeness."

It is one of the most powerful spiritual demonstrations we can make.

And it works.

The Work

Set your intention by saying quietly to yourself or out loud:

> "I am willing to make a list of all I have intentionally or unintentionally harmed. I am willing to be guided by my inner wisdom."

> "I am willing to list anyone toward whom I have a feeling of dis-ease or discomfort."

Contemplate

My willingness to clear up my contribution to a negative situation sets me free.

My willingness to see from another's perspective opens the door to divine understanding.

There's always more than one side to the story. There's my side, the other person's side—and the truth. What's the real truth around the damaged relationships in my life?

Humility is not humiliation. Humility places me in a position of immense power because it removes the attitude of "I'm right and you're wrong," clears out the noise and connects me to the willingness to restore peace no matter whose fault it is. Humility restores my awareness to its original state of truth and love.

I am humbly willing to do anything for my spiritual freedom.

Journal

Revisit your Journal entry for Key Four. Recall the people you identified as sources of difficulty or dis-ease in your life.

- How do you feel about making amends to the people listed in your Key Four?

- How do you feel about your current relationships to these people? Do you feel violated by the idea of making amends if they're the ones who have caused the most harm?

- Is any of this true—or is that just fear talking?

- Even if it is true, and you are not the cause of harm, is being right or being the victim worth holding on to, or are you willing to give that up in order to obtain your freedom and power?

- How far are you willing to go to be restored to wholeness?

Affirmations: Key Eight

I acknowledge the people I have offended based on false beliefs, fear, doubt and unworthiness. I am willing to go to any lengths to clean up my side of the street.

In the realm of Spirit, we are all one—therefore, acknowledging my part in the drama sets us all free.

Action Steps

On a piece of paper, make four columns. In the first column, list the names of people and even institutions (e.g., organizations, banks, the government) that you listed under "resentment" in Key Four. In the second column, refer to the "My Contribution" column associated with that particular name in Key Four, feeling free to add to or clarify as you go. In the third column, under "Amends," list the action steps you're willing to take to set that particular situation or relationship right. In the fourth column, under "I Forgive," list the ways you're willing to forgive yourself for your contribution to this specific issue. *For Example:*

1. *Person*: My Daughter

2. *My Contribution*: I was selfish for only thinking of my wants and needs to be single and free, and not your needs to have a responsible, loving mother. I was dishonest by deluding myself that if I didn't have you, I would have been happier. I was dishonest by thinking I could find love in the arms of a man, instead of having you in my arms.

I was self-seeking by blaming you for my pain and discomfort, and by only thinking about my comfort and not yours.

I feared not having the freedom that I wanted, I had fear about being a horrible mother. I was afraid that if I were a good mother, I wouldn't have enough time for myself. I was afraid of harming you, of not knowing how to treat you the way you always deserved to be treated.

3. *Amends:* I will acknowledge, to my daughter, the part I've played in our painful relationship and take full responsibility for my contribution.

- I will spend loving, quality time with her.
- I will be attentive to her needs and desires from a place of unconditional love, healthy emotional balance and well-being.
- I will commit to always being there for her, forever.

4. *I Forgive*: I forgive myself for not being a good mother. I forgive myself for not knowing how to be present and loving to my daughter. I forgive myself for putting other relationships above my relationship with my daughter. I embrace myself in the loving vibration of Spirit, allowing all of my mistakes to be washed away. I was not a bad person. I was a person operating out of fear, wounds and false beliefs. I am worthy of forgiveness. I forgive myself. I am forgiven. I am enough. All is well.

Closing Thoughts

Have you ever walked into a room and someone was there that you had some negative energy with? Pretty uncomfortable, isn't it? Have you ever bumped into someone that you owed money to, and you haven't taken responsibility for the loan? That's pretty awkward.

As I mentioned earlier, sometimes you can just think about someone and your body will do an involuntary shudder on the inside if there's unclear or negative energy with that person.

I know—it used to happen to me all the time.

But as I became more aware by processing the Keys, those feelings of unclear or negative energy with others became intolerable. "Pain pushes until the vision pulls," meaning we are either motivated to take action because we're so emotionally uncomfortable and have no other choice, or we are inspired by a vision of a better way of living. Well, the pain of bumping into people that I hadn't cleaned up my side of the street with set me straight pretty quickly.

I know, I know—this is a hard one, especially if you feel you're the one who got the raw end of the deal. In the past, before doing the work of this Key, I would kick and scream at the notion that I had to become willing to make amends— especially when "those people" weren't making amends to me. I also experienced the fear of going to those people to do my part of the work because I thought they would judge me or put me down.

However, through practicing the previous Keys, I was tapped into a powerful storehouse of strength and courage to move forward despite my fears.

I've experienced every fear about making amends that you can think of, and I'm the amends queen. So, let me share with you what I've found.

I had to set my intention to detach from the reaction or response of others. I was making amends for my recovery. If they accepted my offerings, great—wonderful. If not—I knew that I had done my very best to make things right, and that fact alone started to restore order to my world.

I gotta tell you, however, that rejection and negativity have never been my experience when making amends, and I've had to apologize for some doozies. I believe Key Eight is spiritually charged by our intentions—to merge more completely with the One Power and Presence that we're part and parcel of—that we are always protected in our efforts. Even while I was making the most challenging amends, I was met with understanding and receptivity. Some people were more open than others, but everyone was willing to hear me out.

This Key kicked my butt into an entirely different stratosphere. It changed my life. I know it will do the same for you.

Meditative Quotes

"Out beyond ideas of wrong-doing and right-doing there is a field. I'll meet you there."

—Rumi

"If we do not move beyond the experience of victimhood, we will stay hopelessly addicted to our woundedness."

—Colin Tipping, *Radical Forgiveness*

KEY 9: CLEANING UP THE WRECKAGE

STEP NINE:
"[We] made direct amends to such people wherever possible, except when to do so would injure them or others."

KEY NINE:
"Backed by all the Power of the Universe, I lovingly, directly and honestly make amends in a way that supports the highest good of all concerned."

Through the Fire

Drug addicts don't like going to work, so I didn't have a good attendance record on any of my jobs while getting loaded. Every Monday or Friday, I'd call in sick.

Well one Monday, while I was still using, I knew the manager wouldn't buy it if I called in sick again. So, during the weekend, there just so happened to be a big fire in Los Angeles that was getting a lot of media coverage. A lot of people died in "The Baldwin Hills Fire." "What a gift," I thought. "I'll tell my job that my sister had died in the fire."

They bought it, and I took off that Monday with no fear of being terminated.

I went back to work the next day like nothing happened. My boss said to me "Ester, what are you doing here?" I had to act the part of a grieving sister, and told her that my sister's body was being flown to New York, and that I couldn't afford to make the trip. I really wanted the matter dropped. I had my day off, and I was cool till next Monday. But they took up a collection for me to fly to New York, for the "funeral."

Well, what was I to do? I had to take the money and take the rest of the week off—a drug addict's dream. An entire week off, with free spending money that was blown in a day to feed my addiction.

Well, today was the day of reckoning. It was time to make amends to my former employer for telling that huge lie, and taking money that wasn't used for what they had intended it to be used for.

On my way to meet with my ex-boss to make amends, my insides were shaking so bad, I had to use the bathroom. I was a mess.

I arrived at the restaurant. She was so glad to see me, but I could barely look her in the face. With my head down and my eyes avoiding her gaze, I began to tell her what I had done. Her eyes became so sad with disappointment, but as I continued to reveal the truth, I became stronger. My head was no longer down, I was looking straight into her eyes, coming clean for the first time in my life.

When I finished, she was very quiet. "Oh, oh," I thought, "she's gonna tell me what I low-life I am."

But she didn't.

When she finally spoke, she said "Ester, I am disappointed, but also very proud of this step you've taken. God bless you, and I forgive you."

I asked her what I could do to make right the wrong I had done, and of course financial restitution was high on the list, but mostly she just wanted me to continue on the path of recovery.

When I left the restaurant, I was no longer Ester, the drug addict, thief, horrible mother and overall bad person. I was an expression of God. It was the first time I actually experienced the presence of God.

I literally felt transparent. I was on fire with unconditional love and joy. I felt a purity that I didn't know existed. I felt cleaner and stronger than I ever had in my life. I felt like myself, a self I had just met but who had been here all along— waiting for me to wake up and come clean.

How It Works

Based on your core wounds and negative patterns, you have caused much harm. Not on purpose, but because that's how you survived.

You lied to protect yourself. You gossiped about others to feel better about yourself, when you actually felt quite small. You rejected and abandoned others because of your habitual pattern of abandoning and rejecting yourself. You dodged your creditors after they were gracious enough to lend you money, because you were afraid of not having enough for your own means if you paid them back. You betrayed people who trusted you, because you continuously betrayed yourself.

You abused people who were depending on you, because you had abused yourself.

Now it's time to make it right.

These actions and the beliefs behind them are like big boulders weighing down your soul, blocking the very good you desire.

"I'm sorry" is not sufficient when action is necessary.

Those you owe reparations to are sure to be more impressed with your demonstration of goodwill than your talk of spiritual discoveries and how sorry you are. Action moves you from theory to practice—from bondage to freedom.

Making amends is not a debate or argument. It is not about telling the person, "I did this because you did that." No—it is about cleaning up your side of the street only. Their side of the street is their business. We do this, and then trust in an orderly Universe to restore our lives—and their lives— to divine harmony and perfect order.

Making amends is an intention to restore order and balance from a place of compassion, love and discernment for all concerned.

Important Note: Step Nine states that we do not make amends if it would only make the situation worse for the person we're apologizing and offering restorative actions to. Be very clear that your intention in this step is not about unloading guilt at the expense of another. For instance, would it really serve your spouse to tell him or her you flirted with someone else last week? Would it serve someone for you to say you've been gossiping about them—unless they already know about it?

The Work

The promise of Soul Recovery requires that we re-interpret events and relationships we have experienced in the past. That is because the stories and interpersonal patterns we have created in the past often do not serve our healing today. Since our past stories were created from a limited set of understandings about our relationship to Spirit, we have the choice between reclaiming and releasing those old stories and patterns—and establishing new ones. The work you have done up to this point has provided space for this process to occur with greater ease.

In our relationships, we have established patterns with the people who have had the most influence over the course of our lives. The process of making amends "renegotiates" our relationship with them, by lovingly and powerfully creating new patterns that serve the highest and best outcome for ourselves and others.

When you have contributed to an unhealthy situation by being selfish, dishonest, self-seeking and afraid, we now understand it is because you felt abandoned, rejected, betrayed, unsafe, etc. (as noted in Key Four). Based on your identity as a spiritual being, I would say that you have subconsciously made spiritual "agreements" or "contracts" with the people you have hurt the most, and who have hurt you the most. You now get to energetically renegotiate a new "contract" with better, more positive terms.

Set your intention by saying quietly to yourself or out loud:

"I face my past mistakes with courage, humility and willingness. Most of all, I face them supported by the love and power of the entire Universe. I am divinely embraced as the shackles of the past fall away from me."

"I forgive myself for the mistakes I've made based on fear and the false vision of myself as less than a perfect expression of Spirit. I am forgiven, I am loved. I forgive myself."

"I energetically renegotiate the painful agreements I have had with people in my life who mirror any false beliefs and negative patterns I have held in consciousness."

Contemplate

It is harder to go to an enemy than a friend, because we fear rejection and judgment. But I remind myself that I am divinely and spiritually protected as I commit to this courageous course of action.

- In order to be restored to wholeness, I must clear away that which makes me feel broken and ashamed.

- When I clean up my side of the street, it clears my mind from feelings of guilt, fear and unworthiness.

- When I clear up the wreckage of my past and present, I release the negative energy that has blocked me from God—my higher self.

By energetically renegotiating my spiritual agreements with myself and the world, I set a new positive law in motion that operates in my life as peace, love, order, integrity, harmony, abundance and joy.

Journal

What shame are you carrying around that you are now ready to release?

How do you feel when you're in the presence of someone you've betrayed, abused, gossiped about, or owe money to?

Do you feel self-righteous, disempowered, ashamed, awkward, fearful?

Are you afraid they will use your admittance of wrong-doing to take advantage of you in the future? Even if they attempted to do so—isn't your freedom and power worth enough to you that you will make amends despite that risk?

Could it be that, because you are now in harmony with the infinite loving intelligence of the Universe, you are protected by this alignment?

How do you think you'll feel once you have cleaned up your side of the street—peaceful, confident, more powerful?

Are you ready to walk with your back straight and your head held high? If so, who are you without all that baggage you've been carrying around?

Affirmations: Key Nine

Backed by all the Power of the Universe, I lovingly, directly and honestly make amends in a way that supports the highest good of all concerned.

In the realm of Spirit, there's only one side of the story, and it is love.

Action Steps

Return to your work from Key Eight. Review each name on the list you generated.

In your journal, write down the incidents or actions for which you need to make amends. Rank each name from 1 to however many names are on your list (for example, let's say 10). Put a 1 next to the person it would be easiest to make amends with; put a 10 next to the most difficult scenario. Continue to rank each name until you have a clear picture of the easiest person or scenario to approach. It's important to start with the easiest reparations first, because every successful instance of making amends and taking actions to clean up your side of the street will help you gain momentum and courage to tackle the next scenario.

In a conversation with your spiritual advisor, decide if you should make contact by telephone, letter, email or face-to-face.

Discern if making amends would implicate others or cause more harm than good. Be totally honest about this. This decision isn't to protect yourself. You are already protected. It's about protecting and honoring others.

Before you approach the person on your list, make an appointment to see your spiritual advisor to get the support you need prior to taking action. Take this opportunity to forgive the person on the list for their wrong-doing in the situation (something you will not be addressing with the actual person), and renegotiate the spiritual agreement that has been made on an energetic level with this person (another area that will not be addressed with the actual person). The purpose of this preparatory work is to make you spiritually and emotionally ready to face the person you're making amends to, and get clarity about the appropriate action to take.

Ask your spiritual advisor to sit in proxy on behalf of the person you're going to be approaching. For the sake of this process, perceive and speak to your advisor as if he/she is the person you'll be making amends to.

For example: you might say something like this, as your spiritual advisor listens deeply:

"I know that my behavior with you has been based on a wounded belief system about myself, and based on that belief system, I have acted inappropriately. I now know the truth about myself and am here to set right any wrong I have done in our relationship. Let me share with you who I really am. I am lovable, loving, brilliant, capable, safe, worthy, deserving and more than enough. I am a perfect expression of God, and I no longer need you to fulfill our old agreement by mirroring back to me my old false ways of being."

"Based on our oneness in Spirit, I am now renegotiating my spiritual agreement with you, and here are my new terms: From this moment on I cease blaming you for my pain and discomfort; I will release you from being responsible for my safety, approval, love and well-being in any way. God is my source. I will tell you the truth no matter what, and allow the spiritual chips to fall where they may.

I will no longer accept disrespectful treatment from you and I will no longer dishonor you. If we are to continue in relationship with each other, I will show up authentically and fully. If it is revealed that being in relationship with each other is not in the highest and best interest for all concerned, I give thanks for the lessons you have taught me and the gifts you have brought me, and release you to your highest and best good. If I owe you money, I will pay you back consistently and honestly in a way that honors everyone concerned."

"I forgive you for anything you have knowingly or unknowingly contributed to the disharmony in this relationship. Thank you for being my angel disguised as my enemy, and for giving me this opportunity for healing and growth. I forgive you. I forgive myself. It is finished. And so it is. Amen."

The above process with your spiritual advisor is essentially "settling spiritual accounts" on an energetic level—something you do prior to having a face-to-face meeting, making a phone call or sending a letter. This same process can be used to address those people on your list who—by your making direct contact—would create more harm than good. Very importantly, this way of making amends is also one of the most powerful ways for you to settle spiritual accounts with someone who has died, or who is physically unavailable to receive your apology.

Once you have engaged in this process with your spiritual advisor for those you will be contacting, you are ready to make the call, set an appointment for a face-to-face meeting, or send an email or letter, and to follow up with appropriate action.

For example, if it was revealed to you in Key Eight that you owe someone money, offer an amount that you can pay weekly or monthly until it is paid in full. If the action step is being more loving, patient and kind to that person, let them know your intentions to do so. If the reparations are to your employer, the action step might be that you will show up for work on time every day and not abuse break time, or that you will show up fully to do the job that is expected of you. If you are sincere in this process, you will know exactly what steps you are to take to set things right.

Will all people be receptive to healing just because you're in this process?

Maybe, maybe not. But if not, it is very important to remember that you are not a door-mat because of the things you've done in your past. You do not deserve to be treated with verbal, emotional or physical abuse. If the person you are making amends to responds with inappropriate anger or action, do not argue—that would defeat the purpose. But you do have permission to take care of yourself by excusing yourself from the situation. If you owe money, send it anyway, but in no way are you to allow another to dishonor or abuse you.

You are an expression of God and worthy of only good.

It is absolutely imperative that you are spiritually centered prior to making amends, and that you have anchored yourself in the work of self-forgiveness and love with your spiritual advisor prior to taking action. Specifically, you might want to review Key Three prior to making amends, as it will give you strength and courage. And remember: you don't have to make amends alone. Allow the Universe—and your spiritual advisor—to support you in this process.

Closing Thoughts

There was a time when I thought this Key was just about setting me free, making my life better. Of course, that is one of the benefits. However, there's a larger purpose for making amends: It is to make ourselves fit to be of maximum service to God—individualized as our fellow man.

We cannot be of service to others if our own side of the street is still in need of repair. When we work through this Key, we can look the world in the eye again; shame and insecurities fall away, and our past becomes our testimony and hope to others in need of spiritual liberation. We also become far more powerful in our ability to serve.

I have made many amends in my recovery. Of course, among those to whom I made apologies and reparations were June Bug and my daughter.

Even though June Bug had made his transition prior to my recovery, I wrote him a letter and went into meditation to connect with his spirit as best I could. I made amends to him for being the initiator of molestation and then lying about it to my parents. I apologized to him, for me and my family treating him like he was an unwanted and unworthy burden. I asked his forgiveness and prayed for his prosperous, loving and peaceful existence in whatever dimension he happens to reside in.

I made amends to my daughter for being so blinded by my wants and needs that I didn't care about hers. I made amends to her for pawning her off on other people when I didn't feel like being bothered. I apologized for not protecting her when she needed me the most. I apologized for not making her feel safe in the love of her mother, and—most importantly—I promised that, from that moment on, she would be a priority in my life and I would be there for her always.

Did June Bug—in whatever dimension he exists—forgive me? I don't know. Has my daughter forgiven me? Sometimes it seems she has, and then sometimes her pain and core wounds take over and she hasn't. Is that my business?

Not really.

My business is to stay true to my commitment of recovery and live up to the amends I've made. My apology to June Bug set me free, and hopefully gave him a sense of peace as well. My commitment to being accountable and present for my daughter allows my heart to remain open and available for when she needs me and wants to come home to my embrace.

Meditative Quotes

"If we are painstaking about this phase of our development, we will be amazed before we are half way through. We are going to know a new freedom and a new happiness. We will comprehend serenity and we will know peace."
—Bill Wilson

"First go and be reconciled to your brother; then come and offer your gift."
—Matthew 5:24

"A man of integrity is a man that follows through with the promises, commitments and agreements that he made with himself and with others. When he does this, he immediately accepts responsibility and takes corrective action."
—Coco Ramos

KEY 10: SPIRITUAL MAINTENANCE

"Relax, Sweetie, you've got the gig."

During my studies at my spiritual community, Agape International Spiritual Center, I had learned that I was not powerless over my circumstances. I learned that the "power greater than myself" was actually the power of God individualized as my true self—and if I used this power affirmatively, I could have a life beyond my wildest dreams.

But even after all these years of being clean and sober, and getting a "new understanding" about God, it was still very difficult for me to accept that my dreams could actually come true—that I was even worthy of my dreams coming true.

But they did!

The voice on the other end of the phone said, "Hello, this is Bette Midler's tour manager, and we were wondering if you would be interested in going on tour with her as a background vocalist, and what your rates might be?"

"What???"

I fell on the floor, thinking this must be some sick joke. "Who is this?" I shouted into the phone.

He repeated his name and told me that Brenda Russell had heard me sing at church and given Bette's music director my name.

Just like that, out of the blue, I was no longer a cracked-out drug addict, or a bitter "watching the clock" legal secretary, no longer a desperate nanny; I was in the green room at the *Oprah* show getting ready to go on stage to sing background vocals for Bette Midler!

I kept asking myself, "Is this real? Okay, when am I going to wake up just to find out this is only a dream?"

I couldn't believe it—and there's Oprah coming into the greenroom to give us all hugs and wish us luck. I think she still had on her bedroom slippers (she only wears "diva heels" while she's on stage).

I was a mess because I was scared to death. I didn't quite believe I deserved to be there. Did they know who I used to be? Did they know I had no idea what the hell I was doing?

I was afraid.

I was afraid that everyone would realize I was a fraud, that I didn't really have any talent. I was afraid someone would pull the coat off my nine-year-old inner child and see the ragged edges of her life, like my sisters did at my fourth grade concert.

Yet, in spite of another layer of unworthiness revealed by this massive event in my life, my dreams were still coming true. Even in the midst of my little girl belief that someone was going to demand I take off my coat and show them my dirty wrinkled clothes, I was a witness to my divinity as an expression of God, and my life being made new.

Bette pinched my arm on the way to the stage and said, "Good luck, sweetie." She really liked me. What did I do to deserve that?

One of Bette's new songs calls for a high note. While we were on stage performing, she pointed to me, and I hit it. All eyes were on me and I was scared to death, but the high note came out with the clarity and beauty of an angel. Spirit was speaking in my ear: "I am forever with you, and all that I have is thine."

My family and friends from home called and congratulated me. They were just as happy as I couldn't seem to allow myself to be. I had one friend say to me, "Ester, relax—you've got the gig."

I am so grateful that in spite of my past, my inner wounds and fears, there remains a power within me that doesn't recognize any of that. It doesn't know me as the dope fiend who walked her daughter to the drug dealer's house at 3 AM, or the young girl who falsely accused her cousin of molestation.

That part of me only knows my wholeness and magnificence—and as long as I keep my spiritual house in order and continue to grow, I can hear it repeating the words of my friend: *Relax, Beloved, you've got the gig.*

How It Works

By the time you get to Key Ten, you have been restored to wholeness to a very large degree. Sometimes it's hard to accept just how much you've changed and it's hard for people who knew the "old" you to accept how much you've grown and changed. Even though you might still struggle with false beliefs about separation from God and unworthiness, you are not the same person you were prior to the beginning of this work—and you've grown so much more than you think you have.

At this point, you may be feeling some spiritual mojo. You're connected and more peaceful than you've ever been. Some amazing gifts are starting to express in your life.

Things are changing.

However, you must be diligent in your spiritual maintenance or when false beliefs rear their heads—and they will—you will lose conscious connection to Spirit, and the fears and feelings of unworthiness will again run the show.

Bill Wilson states in the Big Book: "It is easy to let up on the spiritual program of action and rest on our laurels. We are headed for trouble if we do, for alcohol is a subtle foe. We have a daily reprieve contingent on the maintenance of our spiritual condition."

I'd like to tweak Bill's quote a little bit here by saying that "alcohol" is not the subtle foe you need to look out for, it's your old patterns of thinking and feeling that spin you out of control and set you back.

Even if alcohol or drugs were never your issue, in order to stay connected to your wholeness, you must stay awake through spiritual growth and right action.

Key Ten is a daily practice—a little like automobile maintenance. As soon as something pops up, it's important to take care of it. Don't wait to get all clogged up again. Keep your filters clean and clear, so that you can meet calamity with peace and spiritual equilibrium. Stay in touch and in tune with Spirit so you have the spiritual clarity, dominion and authority to create the life you desire, rather than being held back by your illusions.

Put yourself in a position to rest in oneness with God, No matter what shows up, you'll be able to not only handle it—but to transmute it into harmony and perfect order.

The Work

Set your intention by saying quietly to yourself or out loud:

> "I am awake and aware of my God-self through the spiritual discipline and maintenance of my consciousness. I cherish my freedom as an awakened spirit and will go to any lengths to maintain it."

Contemplate

I am starting to experience a new sense of freedom and peace. I'm feeling more confident and alive. I am consciously connected to Spirit.

I choose to stop battling conditions and appearances— even my addictions. Sanity has been restored. I am whole, perfect and complete.

I've been enough all along. I've been amazing all along. Where I couldn't see before, my inner sight has been restored. I am clear.

This clarity is contingent upon my spiritual maintenance. I will stay alert and aware of any false beliefs, wounds and inappropriate actions, and clean them up through prayer, journaling and making amends where I've caused harm.

Journaling

- What false beliefs and fears have resurfaced at this point?

- What resentments are showing up in your life again?

- Are you willing to clean them up as soon as possible? How?

- What are the wonderful experiences you've had at this point in the process?

- Did you feel fear about your worthiness when these wonderful experiences occurred? What were those fears?

- Did you walk through the fear differently than you would have been able to in the past because of the work you've done so far? How was it different?

- Are you willing to go to any lengths to maintain your new-found freedom and peace?

- What are you waiting for? Get to it!

Affirmations: Key Ten

I am in tune with my inner self. When I am out of alignment with Truth, my intuition informs me, and I listen. I promptly correct my mistakes as they are revealed to me with love, clarity and integrity.

I am a constant gardener of my consciousness. I weed out what no longer serves me and continue to plant seeds of love, worthiness and wholeness. The garden of my mind is a reflection of the mind of Spirit.

Action Steps

Put your hand on your stomach. Feel if you have tension there. That tension is present when you feel fear and anxiety, isn't it? That feeling is your inner child informing you "I'm scared," "I'm not enough," "I'm unworthy," "I'm ugly and fat."

If you are not spiritually conscious (or have not been diligent in your spiritual practice), you will believe these false beliefs—and you will act from that place of misaligned belief.

The process in Key Ten is to take stock of what's going on when feelings of fear or resentment pop up.

Because they will.

When they do, take a short inventory, which includes the amends process if appropriate, and proceed to clean up negative energy. Here's how:

In your journal, set up a page with the date and the title, "Inventory." Below, create four rows: *I'm resentful of, I believe, I fear, Fear-based actions*. See the example for how to use this Inventory Chart to take hold of your emotions and clear up negative energy.

1. *I'm resentful of:* John

2. *I believe*: He smirked when I started to sing.

3. *I fear*: I can't sing, I'm a loser.

4. Fear-based Actions:

- *Selfish*: Only thinking of my wants and needs for approval. Treated John with disrespect because I thought he was judging me

- *Dishonest*: Deluded myself again that I'm not enough

- *Self-seeking* : Put John down to others because I felt bad about myself

- *Afraid*: Afraid of not looking good to my peers.

To make amends: Apologize to John for being disrespectful; Share with him my fears (if appropriate); Go back to Key Three and surrender again.

Be gentle and loving with yourself, beloved. You're doing great.

Clear up any issues that come up in this way. Be sure to check in with yourself periodically, so you don't let too much time go by with out addressing this critical part of your spiritual practice.

You must be diligent about this maintenance—not overly self-conscious, but mindful of when fears, resentments and false beliefs pop up. Your emotional guidance system (inner child) will let you know. He/she is your gut. If you're paying attention, you can't miss it.

Closing Thoughts

The beauty of my experience on *Oprah* was that as terrified as I felt, I had tools to help me through. I had a relationship with Spirit that transcended any belief of unworthiness and fear, and I used that relationship to find strength and success. I must've done twenty Key Ten processes before I ever hit the stage, in addition to having my friends and family pray for me and hold me in a vibration of truth and love.

I gotta tell you, it was a little frustrating to have to do that much work just to get on the stage, but it takes whatever it takes.

Have you ever attempted to clean something that had years and years of grime on it, and one cleaning didn't do the trick? You had to keep cleaning it to really get down to the nitty-gritty? Well, that's where I was—one swipe gets a lot done, but not all of it.

Sometimes we have no clue how deep the old wounds go, or how much we have unintentionally invested in negative beliefs, fears and false identities, until they come up—again.

The good news is you are now awake. You know when you're acting out of fear. You know when you're holding on to resentment and feeling like a victim. You recognize and acknowledge your wounded inner child.

You now have the tools to expose false beliefs and the actions that follow them, clean them up and allow the sunlight of Spirit to restore you again and again—and yes—again!

Meditative Quotes

"The unexamined life is not worth living."
—Socrates

"The breeze at dawn has secrets to tell you. Don't go back to sleep."
—Rumi

"Blessed are the cracked, for they shall let the light in."
—Groucho Marx

KEY 11: CONSCIOUS CONTACT

STEP ELEVEN:
"[We] sought through prayer and meditation to improve our conscious contact with God as we understood Him, praying only for knowledge of His will for us and the power to carry that out."

KEY ELEVEN:
"Through daily prayer and meditation, I deepen my conscious connection to the Divine and experience the fullness of the Universal Presence as the dynamic reality of my life."

The Best High I've Ever Had

Now, I thought smoking crack was pretty amazing at one point in my life, but making conscious contact with God—now that's truly amazing. After the very first time, I was totally hooked.

I really, really wanted to know God more than anything. I used to even write letters to God, asking that God reveal itself to me—like NOW! I would cry and say things like "Where the hell are you?"

By the time I had gotten to the Tenth Step, great changes had taken place in my life, but I was longing for more. I knew there was more. I could taste it. I was longing to return home, yet I didn't even know what or where home was. I didn't remember having been there before, but something in me knew there was a place—a dimension that was awaiting my return—and I wanted to go.

However, when I was informed that meditation was required in order to connect to that dimension, all of my ego conditioning surfaced and I panicked.

"Meditation?" I asked my spiritual advisor. "You mean be quiet—like, totally quiet?"

Privately, I thought to myself, *I'm supposed to release control of my life into the nothingness? AAAAHHHHHH!!!*

My ego—the part of me that would rather die than release control—was traumatized. I was scared to death of the notion that I had to be willing to silence the chatter that was constantly on blast in my head (not that it ever had very much to say).

I'd never been in the silence before. And the thought of it terrified me.

I asked Treva, my sponsor at the time, "What the heck am I gonna do in the stillness?" and she said, "Well, you're gonna be still, Sweetie."

She also said, "Baby, if you really want to know God, you're going to have to meditate."

Well, that did it. I wanted God more than anything in the world. I was fertile soil, ready to be saturated with the living waters of my eternal spirit. To do this, I had to surrender totally, completely and absolutely. I was willing to let go of my little ego if it meant gaining something greater.

So, one evening, I sat in the bathtub listening to a meditation recording from *A Course In Miracles.*

I recited the third step prayer over and over again: "I offer myself to thee."

The next thing I knew, my entire body was writhing in orgasmic ecstasy. I was crying and laughing at the same time. There was white light all around me. All thoughts, concerns and ways I had identified myself fell away. The Universe rejoiced for its beloved had returned home. I felt like I had never left this place, and in truth I hadn't—I just thought I had.

After the tub experience, I called my sponsor because, while I had experienced something beyond anything I could even imagine, I was also scared and I must admit, a little ashamed. I had what I thought was a sexual experience because my entire body had an orgasm. I asked her if I had done something bad. What had just happened to me?

She lovingly calmed me down and said, "That was God, baby—that was God."

I knew then that I had felt the presence of God. Wow—it blew my mind. I became committed on a daily basis to return to the Father's House—God's house within me that had been there all along. It was through prayer and meditation that I got to have a direct connection and hang out with God as much as I wanted to.

How It Works

Everybody's experience isn't going to be as dramatic as the one described in my story.

Some spiritual experiences are quiet and subtle. Others come through the "letter of Spirit," meaning study and contemplation; from an expanded understanding of the nature of the Universe, a spiritual experience happens.

Don't be discouraged if your initial experience of meditation isn't as intense as mine. I don't have an answer for that. Maybe I was so incredibly broken, wounded and under the illusion of separation, that my spiritual experience had to be just as extreme.

We get what we need, in the perfect time and the perfect way. Your experience will be tailor-made just for you.

So, what is meditation exactly?

I believe that the act of meditation is simply a tool to connect with the Divine. I believe it's the most direct tool we have, but a tool nonetheless.

Actual connection to the Divine is the ultimate goal, and when you've made it, you'll know it. It is from that place of connection that your spiritual certainty is non-debatable and non-negotiable. No one can tell you their God is more real than yours, because through your spiritual practice of prayer and meditation, you will have a direct connection to God—no intermediary necessary.

Key Eleven is near the end of our program together because it takes the understanding of the nature of God as outlined in Keys One through Three, and the surrender and spiritual housecleaning in Keys Four through Ten to purify your awareness to the degree that you are now available for your direct contact with Spirit.

Some people meditate to relax or reduce stress. Some people meditate to make their lives better or to support themselves getting through a crisis.

All of that is well and good. When we meditate, we do experience more peace, clarity and calm than ever before, not because God deems us worthy to give us those attributes—but because peace, clarity and calm is the actual nature of God itself.

Meditation helps us feel better because feeling better is a by-product of connecting to the Divine.

However, there will and must come a time when we connect with Spirit for Spirit's sake only. We finally tap into our divinity because it's "home."

And there is no other place we'd rather be.

The Work
Set your intention by saying quietly to yourself or out loud:

> "I am ready to go home through the path of silence. I am ready to release all desires, needs, opinions and judgments, and allow myself to just be. God does the rest."

Contemplate
Meditation transforms our "reasoning" mind into the mind of realization—from thinking and figuring things out, to an intuitive knowing.

In the silence, our mental chatter begins to dissipate, and we connect to our higher selves.

Meditation is the bridge from the material to the divine. It connects me to divine order, harmony, peace, joy, love and abundance. It connects me to Reality.

Journal

How do you feel about quieting your mind and completely letting go of all your concerns, judgments, opinions, needs, desires and worries, and just hanging out in the silence without thinking about anything?

Does it frighten you?

Why?

Have you ever tried meditation before? What was your experience? Are you willing to release your past experience for a new one?

Are you committed to keep at it until you feel the presence of Spirit within your own heart and mind?

If not, why?

There's no judgment here, beloved. I know how difficult this key can be when you've never experienced the profound joy and bliss of "letting go and letting God" run your life before. If you're not quite ready for this Key, go back and read Keys One through Three until you feel safe enough to practice Key Eleven.

Affirmations: Key Eleven

Through daily prayer and meditation, I deepen my conscious connection to the Divine, and experience the fullness of the Universal Presence as the dynamic reality of my life.

Through meditation, I return home to the kingdom of heaven. I celebrate and am celebrated as I touch the realm of reality.

Action Steps

SPIRITUAL FOREPLAY: PREPARING THE
CONSCIOUSNESS FOR SILENCE

Create a quiet place specifically for your prayer and meditation. I find that sitting consistently in one physical location each time you meditate sets up a high spiritual vibration in that space. (Note: This is only suggested, not necessary. You can meditate anywhere.)

If soft music helps to create an ambiance of meditation, go for it. Candles or incense are a wonderful way to make a space feel sacred.

Set the intention to meditate by repeating the following words:

"I set my intention to release all concerns about: [in your journal, list your concerns one by one]."

"I set my intention to release all desires: [list all desires one by one]."

"I set my intention to release all opinions and judgments."

"I set my intention to know, sense and feel the reality and nature of God."

"I set my intention to know, sense and feel my oneness with God."

Take some deep, healing breaths.

Take ten minutes to read something inspirational (which is a great way to prepare your consciousness for silence).

Suggestion: Re-read any one of the Keys or any other book that inspires you. I also have a list of readings in the Resources and References section at the end of this book. For now, here are a few recommendations:

KEY #1—"THE NATURE OF GOD"

The Contemplative Life—Joel Goldsmith

Realization of Oneness—Joel Goldsmith

30 Day Mental Diet—Willis Kinnear

The Wisdom of No Escape—Pema Chodron

Now focus on your breath, the light of the candle, a mantra (a simple phrase you repeat again and again, e.g., "God I offer myself to Thee" or "The Universal Presence and I are One") for five minutes.

Keep bringing your attention back to the breath, candle or mantra when you find your mind wanders to something else—anything else. Gently.

Meditation acts as the bridge to your consciousness connection to Spirit within.

Once your mind is quiet, it's time to pray.

Remember, God is praying the prayer through you, *as you*. You are not praying TO God—you are praying FROM God, AS a unique expression of God.

Affirmative Prayer

Here is an outline of affirmative prayer I have found useful:

Recognition: Speak the nature of God. (See Key One for support.)

Unification: Speak about your oneness with God.

Realization: Speak the subject of your prayer, remembering that in the realm of Spirit, your needs are already met, your desires already fulfilled. It is already done.

Thanksgiving: Give thanks in absolute faith that it (your need met or desire fulfilled) is already done, even if it hasn't shown up yet. You know that your good is on its way.

Release: Let it go. Take your mind entirely off the situation you have prayed about. Release the word just spoken into the divine law, knowing that on time and in perfect time, manifestation will express in tangible form and experience.

Examples of Affirmative Prayer:

God is all that there is—love, peace, harmony, order, joy and wholeness. (Recognition)

This power and presence that I call God is my true identity. There is no separation or otherness. Right where I am
is all the power of the Universe. (Unification)

From this place of oneness with the Divine, I speak my
word for each and every reader and participant of this
work, accepting that right where they are, is the fullness
of God. I know that the power and presence of love is
right now permeating every aspect of their lives, because
it is their very lives. I know that they are restored to their
rightful identities of wholeness, clarity, balance and order.
I know that they have returned home to the Kingdom of
Heaven within. I declare that they are experiencing the
fullness of God as abundance and freedom in their financial affairs, health and emotional well-being in their minds
and body temples. I know that the harmony and order of
God is now operating in their relationships, their offices
and their homes. I accept and declare this truth fully and
completely. (Realization)

I am so grateful and thankful that this reality is now
expressing. (Thanksgiving)

It is done, and so it is. Amen. (Release)

Closing Thoughts

My meditations are certainly not at the level of intensity
described in "My Story" every time I meditate. I must admit,
there were times when I chased that initial experience just
like a drug addict chasing the first high. I didn't understand

that by holding each meditation to the standard of my first experience, I was preventing myself from being fully present for the meditation I was doing at the time.

Each experience is different. There are times when I touch the "hem of the garment" (direct connection to God) and am fully and consciously connected. When I have those experiences, I don't even want to come out of meditation because it's a love and peace that is pure ecstasy. There are other times when I'm twitching, tossing and turning, and can't wait until my twenty minutes are up.

Those are the times I'm in judgment of myself, thinking my meditations are not as effective.

But that's just not so.

Simply by making myself available and making a commitment to put God first, something powerful is always happening.

I've had experiences where I thought I had the worst meditation ever, and then ten minutes after the meditation was over, the answer to a question I had would just pop into my consciousness, or some other miracle was brought forth. It's the Universe's way of telling me, "Judge not according to appearances, but judge with righteous judgment" (John 7:24).

You just do the work. No matter how great or frustrating it may be at times—keep at it.

Spirit will do the rest.

Meditative Quotes

> *"What used to be the hunch or the occasional inspiration becomes a working part of the mind."*
> —Bill Wilson

"Prayer is the avenue through which we make contact, find our oneness, or realize God. Prayer is the means of bringing into our individual experience the activity, the law, the substance, the supply, the harmony, and the all-ness of that which we call God."
—Joel Goldsmith

"Truth is within ourselves...and to know...consists in opening out a way whence the imprisoned splendor may escape...."
—Robert Browning

"Happiness is like a butterfly which, when pursued, is always beyond our grasp, but, if you will sit down quietly, may alight upon you."
—Nathaniel Hawthorne

KEY 12: LOVING SERVICE

KEY TWELVE:
"Through my awakened consciousness, I am now prepared to carry the message of truth out into the world. I am now a clear channel to support the awakening of others to their true identity of wholeness."

Madison Square Garden

I remember attending a concert at Madison Square Garden when I was thirteen years old, sitting in the midst of tens of thousands of fans as we chanted for our idols, The Jackson Five.

All of a sudden, there they were on stage, the lights shining down on them. I was in absolute awe of the creativity and raw talent I saw. It resonated within my entire body because I knew I was looking at an aspect of myself—the part of myself that made me forget about my pain and the world I was living in. The music, lights, action, and sharing my experience with thousands of adoring fans, felt like home to me. I could feel the love and creativity that was coming off the stage—and knew from that moment on, that's what I wanted to do with my life. I had no idea how it could ever happen for me—but I dared to dream.

I dreamed about becoming a star for years. I would fantasize and think about it all the time. As my internal work progressed, I was met with more and more success in my career. At first I considered this to be my dream coming into its own—and it was. But over time, I discovered that a deeper shift was taking place within my awareness.

The thought of fulfilling this dream was no longer just about me. The Keys had prepared me to shift my longing for being a star—for my own sake—to becoming a messenger and inspiration to anyone aspiring to recover their wholeness and live their dreams. I was now ready to be of maximum service to God and my fellows.

The Keys have allowed me to live beyond my wildest imaginings. I stood in awe one evening at the greatness of God, looking out into an audience of tens of thousands of cheering fans, who were holding placards with my name on them—the very stage I had seen the Jackson Five on so many years before—at Madison Square Garden.

I have not only performed at the actual venue, Madison Square Garden, five or six times within the past several years but, because of practicing and embodying the Keys one day at a time (and sometimes even one minute at a time), I've been blessed to have had many "Madison Square Garden Moments" in these past twenty-five years of sobriety.

The most important healing has been the healing of my self-worth and the recovery of my integrity and dignity. I no longer walk into a situation wondering, "Why would

somebody like me?" or "Don't they know who I used to be?"
I can now walk into any situation knowing that I am a perfect
expression of God—even with all my flaws.

I am truly enough.

I can hold my daughter in my arms and be fully present
as her mother. As I continue to forgive my past, she forgives
me too. Spirit has restored the lost years, as I get to be a conscious, awake and loving grandmother to my beautiful grandson, Ethan.

I no longer hit up the AM/PM Mini Mart at midnight
with Krispy Kreme donut glaze running down my chin. The
eating disorder that was a counterpoint to my drug addiction
is now in a state of healing—as long as I stay connected and
awake to my oneness with Spirit.

I get to speak all over the world and talk about how my
old, painful story has been transformed into a new, loving and
powerful story of grace, fulfillment and success. I am humbled
by the souls who come to me for help, who see something in
me that they want for themselves.

And to know that they have it too, because it's already
within them.

It has been a long road of recovery, From drug addiction
and all the attendant feelings of low self-worth and self-sab-
otaging behaviors, to standing where I am today. It has taken
everything I have to be restored to wholeness, balance and a
sense of peace.

As you read the story of my rebirth from the ashes of
a desolate and tragic life, and practice the tools outlined in
this book, I promise that you will get to the other side and
find love, peace and wholeness in your life. You are then in

a position to share your testimony with those who want to experience what you now have.

How It Works

Remember when I said in Key Nine that we are committed to this spiritual journey not only for our freedom, but to become fit instruments to carry this message and hope to others who are suffering?

There are people—right now—suffering from being stuck in their wounds and old stories. They suffer from the core belief that struggle, pain, sickness and disease are normal ways of being in the world.

It is through the process you have engaged in over the past 12 weeks that you get to awaken from the nightmare of illusion into the realm of reality—where nothing needs to be fixed, because nothing is actually broken; Where nothing can be improved, because it is already perfect. It is a state of awareness where struggle is not reality, because all that is needed and desired is already given.

It is by taking this courageous and sometimes arduous stand that you line up in consciousness with your freedom, peace, balance, abundance, health and wholeness.

But it is not for you alone.

You have taken this path to be a light for those in darkness, a path for others to find their way. In a sense, you are indeed your "brother's keeper."

There are times when helping another is the very thing needed to—as Ralph Waldo Emerson wrote—"get your bloated nothingness out of the way." Turning your attention away from your own stuff and seeking someone out who you can support is one of the most effective ways of restoring your life to balance and order.

Evangelism is not necessary or advised. The people you will serve will feel the sincerity and power of your walk better than hear your talk of how spiritual you are—and they will seek you out.

The message of these principles will serve the right people at the right time. Don't lose the opportunity to serve at a later time by trying to force these principles on someone not yet ready to receive them.

It's not just being of service that matters, it's *how* you serve. Service is not about trying to fix anyone, or do everything for them. It's about serving in the most effective way, and making available to those you serve the spiritual tools that helped you, so that they may walk towards their own healing.

You are now in position to truly love your neighbor through loving yourself.

The Work

Set your intention by saying quietly to yourself or out loud:

I am available to serve. I am a channel of divine love, clarity and order. I am the sermon others will see.

Contemplate

My pain can transform into my testimony and be a healing light for others.

Through transformation, I am living proof to others that God is real and is always conspiring for my highest good.

In order to be an inspiration to others, I must first clean
my own house—and keep it clean to the best of my ability.

Journal

If you have been practicing discipline and consistency with
the Keys, there have been some major shifts in your life. What
are they?

Can you see how your experience, pain, growth and transformation can benefit others?

How?

In what ways are you willing to serve others?

Are there ways of serving that excite you?

Are the ways you serve making you feel overwhelmed,
used, afraid or joyful, fulfilled and peaceful?

Affirmations: Key Twelve

Through my awakened consciousness, I am now prepared to carry the message of truth. I am available to support the awakening of others to their true identities as
expressions of Spirit.

I am divinely guided and directed as to where, who and
how to serve. I don't choose who I will help—The Universe
leads, and I follow.

Action Steps

Take out a piece of paper, and write down all the important
challenges you have faced during the process you have engaged
in over the past 12 weeks. Be sure to include those challenges
you have not yet resolved, but that are still in process.

Each entry on your list represents a potential way to contribute in service to other people. Each entry shows how you were able to transcend a real and sometimes profound problem. Most of these represent significant work and effort on your part. You have walked this path, and either found a solution, or are actively working on one.

These are incredibly powerful tools in the right hands.

As you look at the list, consider which entries call to you as a means to serve others. Consider which ones have organizations or affiliations that you could contact for the purpose of serving.

What and where is the greatest need?

Then, contact people and organizations you can serve. Start by volunteering.

The power of this intention will bring people and situations into your life, so stand ready to be of service when called upon.

Be sure to remember that service is not about being taken advantage of. We serve others so that eventually, they can help themselves. Be mindful of that.

Stretch beyond your comfort zone by serving in a capacity you're not accustomed to. The transformational nature of service is fulfilled when we are operating at our peak potential, which we do not achieve by "playing it safe."

Closing Thoughts

Service is one of the most powerful spiritual practices for those of us who have spent our lives thinking only of ourselves. Being of service expands your consciousness and your world. It breaks the false belief that "it's all about you," and awakens your awareness to the fact that it's about all of us.

It's not easy for most people who suffer from addictions to "get out of themselves" and think about others. I know it wasn't and isn't for me, but I do it anyway—and feel an instant connection to the Universe when I do. When I seek out others to serve, I am simultaneously releasing resistance to whatever is happening in my world, thus allowing the will of Spirit to be done through me.

Isn't that what it's all about anyway?

Meditative Quotes

"No matter how far down the scale we have gone, we will see how our experience can benefit others. That feeling of uselessness and self-pity will disappear. We will lose interest in selfish things and gain interest in our fellows."
—Bill Wilson

"Give a man a fish and you feed him for a day.
Teach a man to fish and you feed him for a lifetime."
—Chinese Proverb

CONCLUSION

Congratulations! You have done a lot of work in these past twelve weeks, demonstrating your willingness to go to incredible lengths for your wholeness and freedom.

The process of Soul Recovery is one that lives in us every day. The practice is a constant stream of awakening, acknowledging, surrendering and releasing—followed by appropriate action. This occurs on multiple levels, with multiple issues, in all of the various relationships we find ourselves in.

After doing this work, I have found that my thinking no longer defaults to the belief that life is "having its way" with me—but actually is presenting me with obvious choices throughout my day and my week. I have found that in practicing the spiritual tools outlined in this book, I have developed the confidence to follow through with the higher choices I make. That was not always the case. The quality of our life is always about what we choose in the moment. We can live in heaven or hell—but it is determined by what we decide about life and our relationship to it.

I've always said that to engage in Soul Recovery, you must be a spiritual warrior, because it requires heart—your whole heart and commitment to explore those places that have heretofore been too painful to deal with. It takes loving yourself beyond what you knew you were capable of in order to bring old habits and wounds to the surface of your conscious mind and offer them to Spirit for healing.

And you've done it!

I'm so proud of you because I, of all people, know what it takes. I too have had to die in order to be reborn—over and over again.

This is a life-long process. It doesn't end because you've done twelve weeks of deep healing work, but as you continue to purify your consciousness, I promise you that it gets easier and clearer. You now have an opportunity to really live your life rather than allowing yourself to be beat up by your illusion about life.

Life is good. It's always been good. There's never been anything "out there" that had it in for you. The only thing that's ever been against you, my friend—is you.

Now that you have experienced transformation and healing, you can become your biggest advocate through your own thinking and co-creation with Spirit. The Universe— God, nearer than your hands and feet, closer than your very breath—desires to express unlimited joy, love, peace, and wholeness through you.

It is after all, who you really are.

Spirit can only do for you what it does *through* you. You've now become a clear channel so that God can express what It's always been expressing—being magnificent AS you!

Oh, what a beginning you've made. Keep up the good work, and remember that you will never walk alone—ever again.

I love you,
Ester

ACKNOWLEDGMENTS

I would first and foremost like to give thanks to the divine presence of God for expressing through me as the courage to expose myself in all my glory—the good parts as well as those parts of myself sometimes difficult to face. I've come to believe that those parts that I'm not proud of can serve a higher purpose by transforming into teachings that are powerful, loving and effective.

Challenges often become our greatest strengths.

Second, this book simply would not have happened without the vision, persistence, brilliance and love of my best friend, producer, manager and co-writer of this book, Ben Dowling. Ben, thank you for stretching and pushing me to unfold into the greater idea of Spirit as the author of my first book when I wanted to dig in my heels and argue until I was blue in the face. You didn't give up on me—you never have. Thank God for that!

Michael Bernard Beckwith, thank you for guiding me from a place of powerlessness to power, authority and dominion over my own life by anchoring me in awareness that God is not only where I am, but *is* what I am. Thank you.

A special thank you to Stephen Powers of Agape Media International and Hay House for believing in this project. I truly appreciate you.

I'd like to thank Kaia Van Zandt for expanding my vision and seeing the possibility for this book even before I did. Thank you, Rebecca Heyman, for being an excellent, creative editor. You didn't have the opportunity to put up with my occasional stubbornness and fear—Ben was the loving recipient of all that. Thank you, David Sherwood, for brainstorming with me and your endless support.

Blessings and thanks to Wanice Mattola, Suzi Lula and Cynthia James for praying me through when I couldn't see my own way through.

A very special thanks to Treva Wilson and Gary Post who—twenty-five years ago—held my hand, took me to meetings, walked me through the 12 Steps and stayed on the phone with me for hours, as I cried and prayed to stay sober. You allowed me to sit on your doorstep and wait for you to come home from work, so that I could just hang out with you—because I was too afraid of my own shadow to be alone. You carried me until I learned to walk, and I will never forget it.

Thank you, Mila Gutgartz, for loving me through the fire.

I'd like to thank my daughter, Shawntee, for being the greatest gift of love in my life. Even though I've said it a thousand times before, I want you and the world to know how special you are and how much I adore you. You are my constant love, no matter what, and I am yours—no matter what. Thank you for bringing our boy Ethan into the world.

Finally, I'd like to thank my father, the late Reverend Buck V. Rogers, for being the only safe place I had to land when I was a child. For, even in what the world calls death, I still feel your love and protection. I love you, Daddy.

Thank you, all of my friends who cheered me on and witnessed me grow to where I am today. I love you so much, and promise to keep on doing the work—which is never truly done.

ABOUT THE AUTHOR

Ester Nicholson is an Agape-licensed spiritual therapist, recovery coach and inspirational recording artist who brings her personal experience of 25 years of sobriety coupled with a committed practice of spiritual principle to audiences around the globe—with riveting keynotes, soul nurturing music, transformative workshops and powerful teaching programs.

For the past 17 years, she has studied under Michael Bernard Beckwith, the founder of Agape International Spiritual Center and a featured teacher in the book and motion picture, *The Secret*. A gifted vocal artist with her own national releases, Ester has completed two world tours with Rod Stewart and Bette Midler, in addition to appearing on such television shows as *Oprah*, *The Tonight Show*, *The View*, *Good Morning America*, *The Ellen DeGeneres Show* and many others.

Ester is currently touring internationally, teaching and facilitating workshops, giving keynote addresses to organizations and companies—all of which incorporate principles from *Soul Recovery: 12 Keys to Healing Addiction*, her 12-week course of study based on the 12-Step process.

Ester also publishes *SoulRecovery.org*, a web site and newsletter that delivers powerful practices, tools, processes and inspiration to people in recovery of all kinds.

RESOURCES AND REFERENCES:

Soul Recovery Web Site

The purpose of this book is to serve those who are most in need of healing in the area of addiction and dependence. Due to the needs of that community, I've created a web site for providing timely and updated resources and reference materials. These materials are provided free for all.

On the site you will find links to important resource sites, curriculum and teaching materials, workshop information, downloadable materials and a means to contact a growing network of *12-Key* coaches and therapists.

You can access that site here:

http://www.soulrecovery.org

Once on the Home Page, I recommend that you create an "account" to have full access to the web site. There is no charge for this access. When I have something important to share, I will send an email out with information to you including: my schedule of workshops in your area, teacher training information for those interested in developing a 12-Key coaching practice, and more.

Social Media

In addition to the web site, I also have presence on both Twitter and Facebook that is updated much more frequently. I invite you to join me as this important work unfolds:

Twitter: *@soulrecovery*
Facebook: *http://www.facebook.com/soulrecovery*

Reading List

Over the years, I have found great inspiration and value in the following books:

The Big Book of Alcoholics Anonymous - Bill Wilson
Radical Forgiveness - Colin Tipping
Radical Self-Forgiveness - Colin Tipping
Realization of Oneness - Joel Goldsmith
The Contemplative Life - Joel Goldsmith
The Art of Meditation - Joel Goldsmith
The Power of Now - Eckhart Tolle
Inner Bonding - Margaret Paul, Ph.D.
Spiritual Liberation - Michael Bernard Beckwith
The 30 Day Mental Diet - Willis Kinnear
The Wisdom of No Escape - Pema Chodron
The Abundance Book - John Randolph Price
In The Meantime - Iyanla Vanzant
Peace from Broken Pieces - Iyanla Vanzant
Ask and It Is Given - Esther and Jerry Hicks (Abraham)
Science of Mind Textbook - Ernest Holmes
For The Inward Journey - Howard Thurman
Quiet Talks With the Master - Eva Bell Werber

Author Web Site

For additional information, or to contact me for bookings, workshops and performances, please feel free to connect through my personal web site at:

http://www.esternicholson.com

MY SOUL RECOVERY JOURNAL

What I am and have, the world did not give
and the world cannot take away.

MY SOUL RECOVERY JOURNAL

I release blaming others for my pain or holding anyone outside
myself accountable for my fulfillment, joy, love or my safety.

MY SOUL RECOVERY JOURNAL

Time does not heal all wounds. Time scabs over wounds. Prayer,
meditation and forgiveness heal—restoring me to sanity.

MY SOUL RECOVERY JOURNAL

It is not done unto me as I say, it is done unto to me as I believe. I
believe that God is good and I am now one with my good.

MY SOUL RECOVERY JOURNAL

My beliefs and thoughts are in service to highest
good and not my past illusions.

MY SOUL RECOVERY JOURNAL

Wherever I find myself, I have consciously or unconsciously prayed myself into being here. If I don't like where I am, I have options.

MY SOUL RECOVERY JOURNAL

I release fighting anything or anyone.